MARABI NIGHTS

early south african jazz and vaudeville

MARABI NIGHTS

early south african jazz and vaudeville

christopher ballantine

Ravan Press
Johannesburg

First published by Ravan Press
PO Box 31134 Braamfontein 2017
South Africa

© Christopher Ballantine 1993

All rights reserved. No part of this publication may be reproduced, stored in a retrieval system, or transmitted in any form or by any means, electronic, mechanical, photocopying, recording, or otherwise, without the prior permission of the copyright owners.

First published 1993
Second impression 1994

ISBN 0 86975 439 4

Cover design: Monica Seeber, Ravan Press
DTP setting and design: Ravan Press

The financial assistance of the Centre for Science Development (HSRC, RSA) towards the publication of this work is hereby acknowledged. Opinions expressed in this publication and conclusions arrived at are not necessarily to be attributed to the Centre for Science Development

Printed by Kohler Carton & Print (Natal)

To the memory of my father
Ronald Ballantine,
scientist, musician and mentor:
whose deeply intelligent curiosity about the world
was always such a powerful inspiration
– and who died shortly before the completion of this book.

Contents

Preface ix
Acknowledgements xi

MARABI NIGHTS
Memory, History and Context:
An Introduction and Overview 1

CONCERT AND DANCE
The Foundations of Black Jazz in
South Africa Between the 1920s and the Early 1940s 11

MUSIC AND EMANCIPATION
The Social Role of Black Jazz and Vaudeville
in South Africa Between the 1920s and the Early 1940s 39

MUSIC AND REPRESSION
Race, Class and Gender in Black South African
Jazz Culture up to the Early 1940s 63

Appendix 87
Index 102

Preface

I cannot imagine American jazz without the 'Hot 5' and 'Hot 7' Louis Armstrong recordings of the 1920s. How would we understand the music if we were somehow ignorant of the historical circumstances and cultural milieu of its early development? Would we still be searching for the 'lost chord' (or blue note) of American identity?

The equivalent in South African jazz – its early history – has largely been forgotten. The music, the musicians and the social setting of early South African jazz and vaudeville remain only in memory and in a few treasured collections of old recordings. However, in *Marabi Nights* the long tradition of 'jazzing' is revealed.

The post 'Graceland' era – from the mid-1980s – has seen various forms of local South African music emerge on the international stage. However, in the 1960s and 1970s South Africa was, musically speaking, better known for its 'exile' jazz musicians, while jazz players living in the country were largely unknown.

What cultural forces impelled world-renowned artists like Hugh Masekela, Abdullah Ibrahim and Chris McGregor to become jazz musicians in the first place? The existence of a long local jazz tradition will come as news to many. As Christopher Ballantine points out in his introduction, 'most of the recordings on the cassette that accompanies this book have not been publicly available – probably have not even been heard for more than 50 or 60 years'. Neither has there been a comprehensive history to read; no Gunther Schuller, LeRoi Jones or Alan Lomax to exhume and analyse the musical evidence.

Ballantine's work on the pre-history, evolution and early days of South African jazz required years of research and interviews with musicians unheard of for decades. It necessitated combing through hundreds of back issues of popular magazines and newspapers, tracking down out-of-print 78s and selecting key examples from hours and hours of music. All of this had to be done before page one of *Marabi Nights* could be written.

Christopher Ballantine's book is far more than a valuable academic study. It makes available the first historical perspective on a range of issues which are extremely urgent and emotive in transitional South Africa. These issues are the exploitation of black musicians by commercial interests; the racial politics of white and black musicians' unions; the debate within the African National Congress (and the Left generally) about the role of music in the liberation struggle and subsequent reconstruction; the depth and degree of American influences; the 'dream' of professional music education taking place within the black community; gender, class and race dynamics; and, very importantly, the genesis of *mbaqanga*. These are precisely the 'hot topics' of the 1990s, often the subject of debates which generate more heat than light.

Turning to the music on the tape, the influence of these early pioneers can still be heard in contemporary popular music. Musicians and commentators alike will be fascinated to discover these roots.

Marabi Nights is a very significant work. It is the book I have been waiting for since my arrival in South Africa in 1983. It is a milestone in the literature of black South African music and will remain so. Cultural emancipation can only be achieved with critical insight and historical self-knowledge. This book has shown the way to both. As they say in the jazz clubs, 'heita!' (we want more!).

Darius Brubeck
Director
Centre for Jazz and Popular Music
University of Natal, Durban

Acknowledgements

This book could never have been written without the unstinting co-operation of many of those who played, sang, danced, or simply watched and listened, wherever *marabi*, vaudeville and jazz were performed in South Africa's towns and cities in the years before the early 1940s. Though they are too numerous to mention individually, I must single out a few whose contributions were of exceptional significance.

Top of the list is Peter Rezant, doyen of South African popular music, and now one of the last survivors of that fabulous generation of musicians who held the country's urban black population in thrall during the early decades of this century. Peter has been more generous with his time, and is possessed of a more precise and encyclopaedic memory, than any researcher making use of oral history has a right to expect. Others I must mention by name are Lindi Makhanya, the late Wilson Silgee, Louis Petersen, and Ntemi Piliso (at 68 years of age, the youngster in this list). The recent and belated 'rediscovery' of Ntemi – though largely as a performer of music whose roots are of more recent vintage than the music I discuss here – symbolizes my deepest hope for this book: that it will contribute to the recovery of a forgotten cultural and musical history, and thus assist – in its own modest but appropriate way – in the enormous task of cultural reconstruction that awaits all of us who hope for a free and democratic South Africa.

Informants aside, thanks are also due to others who have contributed to the book and the long period of research that preceded it. I warmly acknowledge the assistance of Rob Allingham, who placed his expert discographical knowledge at my disposal, and helped generously with a number of technicalities relating to the preparation of the accompanying cassette. While this book forms part of an ongoing research project of my own, it is also part of a much larger commitment made by the Department of Music at the University of Natal to the study of the past, present and future of music in South Africa. I am indebted to all the colleagues, students and friends who have discussed its ideas with me or contributed in other ways. I think particularly of Veit Erlmann, Lara Allen, Diana Simson (who remains my most perceptive and discerning critic), and the late Bongani Mthethwa. But I wish also to mention Darius and Cathy Brubeck, Jürgen Bräuninger, Dale Cockrell, Anne Pretorius and Max and Delayne Loppert.

Andrew Tracey and the staff of the International Library of African Music, at Rhodes University, made available to me their precious resources. Themba Mbhele, Tobeka Ramncwana and Roy Letsekha produced admirable translations, often from worn, scratched and scarcely decipherable 78 r.p.m. gramophone records.

When my work on this project first began, Tim Couzens, Eddie Koch and Tom Nkadimeng were helpful in a variety of ways; much later, when the book went into production, Ingrid Obery and Monica Seeber at Ravan Press saw it through with an unusual combination of care and efficiency. Evelien Hagen's contribution is hard to specify: amongst other things, she enriched my life, lightened my load.

My research has been supported by grants from the Centre for Science Development (who also made a contribution to the publication costs) and the University of Natal. But the views expressed in this book, and the conclusions it arrives at, are of course my own.

Christopher Ballantine
June 1993

MARABI NIGHTS

Memory, History and Context: An Introduction and Overview

In the rich panoply of black urban popular musical traditions in South Africa, the 'jazzing' tradition lays claim to a special place. This jazzing style has a history vibrantly stretching back to the early years of the century but also bears the traces of even older sources; it has a history of openness to change and to creative engagement with other styles but also of fierce battles around such issues; it has a history shaped by, but also shaping itself in resistance to, the fundamental social and political stakes of a deeply repressive and exploitative social order. And its range of musical idioms has been a repository for some of the country's finest creative energies, now increasingly being celebrated internationally. In short, the jazzing tradition can claim credentials which define its makers as bearers of one of South Africa's proudest cultural heritages. With such credentials, the history of this tradition would, in any healthy society, have become an established part of popular cultural knowledge and listening experience.

But this has not come to pass (for South Africa is no healthy society). In fact, outside a small circle of specialists,[1] virtually nothing is known – or, at least, remembered – about the history of this remarkable

---

[1] Some recent scholarship has begun, slowly, with difficulty, and always on the margins, to reconstruct the history of urban black performance culture in South Africa: Such works as Veit Erlmann's *African Stars: Studies in Black South African Performance*, Chicago 1991, Charles Hamm's *Afro-American Music, South Africa, and Apartheid*, New York 1988, and David Coplan's *In Township Tonight! South Africa's Black City Music and Theatre*, Johannesburg 1985 are obvious examples.

music. Its sounds are silent; its erstwhile heroes are dead or dying in oblivion.

It is into this relative void that this book proposes to step, by setting out to focus on the music's 'beginnings' – if I can put it that way – during the early decades of this century. For it was then that the black jazzing subculture in South Africa was inventing, developing and perfecting styles of music, musical performance, and dance – without which many of the South African musics so revered today would never have come about, and without a knowledge of which they cannot properly be explained or understood. In that sense, then, these early decades produced music which, though it was an end in itself that did not await any later completion, served as a foundation for a range of subsequent developments.

But the status of these decades as the founding years is not the only reason for considering them on their own. There are other grounds, too, for thinking of them as a distinctive era within the evolution of South African jazz culture, and for demarcating them from those that follow. The music of these years, and the practices that surround it, were informed by a set of concerns in many ways different from those that inform the music and practices of the years after the early 1940s. The changing social and material circumstances of the 1940s inaugurated not only new, radical styles of political will and organisation, but also styles of jazz touched by a new self-awareness which differed from the more liberal forms and outlook of the earlier years.

There is a further, and quite distinct, reason for singling out the music of the early decades for separate discussion and listening. Though urban black popular music in South Africa today inevitably carries traces of the musical styles that preceded it, it is profoundly and scandalously amnesic of its own history. While no-one today listens any longer to the extraordinary music of a 1950s 'superstar' group such as the Manhattan Brothers, for some the name will still at least kindle a distant memory; but in the case of (say) the 1930s or early 1940s the names of great and seminal composers and performers such as William Mseleku, Snowy Radebe, Solomon Cele, or Griffiths Motsieloa typically cannot raise even a flicker. To be sure, the depth of this amnesia is inseparable from the fact that most of the recordings on the cassette that accompanies this book have not been publicly available – probably have not even been *heard* – for more than 50 or 60 years.

But the roots of the problem go deeper. Any attempt to recover the music of those earlier years – certainly this is true of the period before 1950 but in many instances it applies to the period after it as well – is profoundly complicated by the scandalously irresponsible attitude to-

Memory, History and Context

wards its preservation displayed by institutions that ought to have known better: in particular, the record companies and the South African Broadcasting Corporation (SABC). For example, Gallo (Africa), as it is now known, though one of the major players on the South African commercial recording scene since 1930, does not possess an archival collection of the thousands of records of urban black popular music the company produced or sold before the 1950s.[2] And the SABC, according to reliable sources within the organisation, simply disposed of vast quantities of this music when the corporation moved to its new premises in Auckland Park – evidently on the instructions of senior executives who believed those recordings were no longer of interest to anyone.

From this vantage point, we should not be surprised by the amnesia that bedevils a popular understanding of the history of black South African jazz. For not only was the community that produced and shared in this music always excluded from meaningful control over the usual institutions of preservation and dissemination (recording studios, radio, and so on), but its exclusion took the form of a double alienation: by class and by race. Among institutions, only the International Library of African Music in Grahamstown and the Department of Music at the University of Natal have made a serious effort to acquire and preserve substantial collections of commercially recorded urban black popular music of real historical value. And though these are, perhaps, the most important institutional holdings of this music – not just in South Africa but indeed anywhere in the world – even they are far from complete.

This book covers one aspect of a single era in the history of South African popular music. But just as *marabi*, early jazz and vaudeville can be understood only in relation to the social context that gave them birth, so also they were never wholly distinct from the various musical traditions that preceded, surrounded and finally followed them. A basic knowledge of these traditions would be a useful starting point for the specific and detailed study in subsequent chapters. However, for the variety of reasons I have outlined, no such knowledge – not even of some of the features central to an understanding of South African music – can be assumed.

---

2 The appointment by Gallo (Africa) of the outstanding discographer Rob Allingham to a newly-created post of archivist in 1990, was a laudable – if belated – attempt to made some amends. A number of reissues, principally of music from the 1950s and 1960s, have already appeared since his appointment. These belong to the period in which, for the first time, studio recordings were made directly onto electro-magnetic tape – and it is these that today constitute the earliest recordings in the Gallo archive.

From Minstrels to Isicathamiya

If there is one concept which is fundamental to any understanding of urban black popular music in South Africa, it is that this music is a fusion – vital, creative, ever-changing – of traditional styles with imported ones, wrought by people of colour out of the long, bitter experience of colonisation and exploitation. The colonisers brought not only guns (for the heathen flesh) and bibles (for the soul), but – with equal pride – the trappings of an entire culture, including its leisure activities. In nineteenth-century South Africa (to go back no further than this), one of the most important of these turned out to be the minstrel show. Records suggest that white minstrels wearing 'black face' were performing in Cape Town as early as 1848; by the 1860s, certainly, more famous American troupes had arrived by ship in Durban and Cape Town. Abetted no doubt by its inherently racist overtones, black-face minstrelsy enjoyed huge popularity among white audiences.

Blacks encountered the genre from the start and, like American blacks, soon tried to capture it for their own ends. By 1880, at least one African minstrel troupe was performing in Durban, and by the turn of the century the fashion had penetrated even to remote rural areas, where Africans formed troupes with names like the Pirate Coons or the Yellow Coons. By then, however, black American minstrels were intoning spirituals and singing of the 'O Happy Days' to come when people will have 'Turned Back Pharoah's Army, Hal-el-u!' Several such groups, now calling themselves 'jubilee' singers, visited South Africa during the 1890s. They left a legacy that reverberated deeply in the consciousness of Africans. Most famous of the visitors – and most beloved of local black audiences – were Orpheus McAdoo and the Virginia Jubilee Singers, who toured nationally and made no fewer than six visits to Durban and Natal alone.

McAdoo – as a model of what 'Africans in America' could achieve – was a hero. African choirs modelling themselves on his group sprang up rapidly. Important in their repertoire were spirituals: Africans were moved by the expression, in these songs, of a longing for justice, freedom and a universal fraternity of humankind.

If the realisation of their hopes was continually to be deferred, Africans continued anyway to create cultural practices in which such aspirations could constantly be rekindled; and some of these, at least, continued also to resonate with the memory of nineteenth-century minstrelsy. From the late 1920s, for instance, workers in the coal-mining districts of the Natal midlands began forging an extraordinary performance style, vibrantly alive with echoes of American minstrelsy, spirituals, missionary hymnody, Tin Pan Alley and Hollywood tap-dance (admired by black workers since the early films of Fred Astaire), as well as Zulu traditional idioms. Commonly known today as *isicathamiya*, this is the genre that has in recent years captured international attention through the work of Ladysmith Black Mambazo.

Isicathamiya – or *mbube* (lion), as it was often called, after the title of a 1939 hit record in the style – is inseparable from the history and struggles of the Zulu-speaking working class. Often it has been frankly political – not only because of its lyrics, but also by virtue of its links to workers' organisations. Most recently, for instance, *isicathamiya* choirs have regularly sung at mass rallies organized by the Congress of South African Trade Unions (Cosatu). But the fertile seeding ground of *isicathamiya* survives wherever Zulu migrant workers are thrown together in hostels in industrial centres, and its robust and ravishing creations are still proudly displayed – as they have been for decades – in weekly allnight competitions in dingy hostel or township halls. Ladysmith Black Mambazo are simply the most famous of the *isicathamiya* groups. Or perhaps not so simply, for at least in part they owe their fame to the government-controlled SABC which, since the 1960s, has enthusiastically broadcast their recordings because their lyrics tend to be metaphorical and religious, rather than overtly critical of the social order.

Marabi, Early Jazz and Vaudeville up to the mid-1940s[3]

Isicathamiya is arguably the most important purely vocal style to have emerged in South Africa this century. But by no later than the First World War, an original instrumental music of perhaps even greater significance – and ultimately far greater renown – was being refined in the black city ghettoes, especially those in Johannesburg. This was *marabi*, a style forged principally by unschooled keyboard players who were notoriously part of the culture and economy of the illegal slumyard liquor dens. A rhythmically propulsive dance music, *marabi* drew its melodic inspiration eclectically from a wide variety of sources, while harmonically it rested – as did the blues – upon an endlessly repeating chord sequence. The comparison is apt: though not directly related to the blues, *marabi* was as seminal to South African popular music as the blues was to American. (The cyclical nature of each, incidentally, betrays roots deep in indigenous African musics.)

---

[3] It is the music discussed in this section that is of course the central focus of this book. The chapters that follow deal with it almost exclusively; and the cassette accompanying this book presents appropriate selections chosen from the phonograph recordings of the time. A detailed discussion of the music on the cassette can be found in the Appendix.

Marabi Nights

For almost everyone not condemned to life in the ghetto, *marabi* and its subculture was evil: associated with illegality, police raids, sex, and a desperately impoverished working class, it was vilified as a corrupting menace. It is no surprise, then, that not a single one of the many early *marabi* musicians was ever recorded. In the absence of recordings of early *marabi*, the fading memories of a few survivors – musicians, or those who watched, danced or listened – have become crucially important. The most illustrious *marabi* musicians of the era before and after 1920 are all dead; Ntebejana, Boet Gashe, Toto, Highbricks, or Nine Fingers, for example, can no longer tell their own stories.

American influences on black city culture – present of course long before the 1920s – found new outlets during and after the 1920s, notably through the sale of gramophones, American-made records, and American films. By the late 1920s and early 1930s, black dance bands started to appear, modelling themselves directly on American prototypes. Soon there was a profusion of such bands and they played not only American (or American-inspired) swing numbers, but also – and more significantly – their own *marabi*-based pieces in swing style. It is this unique and prodigious genre that later came to be known as African jazz or *mbaqanga*. Symbols of what black people could achieve in a white-dominated world, swing bands flourished, and played to capacity crowds in ramshackle township halls around the country. The best of them – the Jazz Maniacs, the Merry Blackbirds, the Rhythm Kings, the Jazz Revellers, the Harlem Swingsters – achieved country-wide fame.

But the bands were not alone. Existing beside them – indeed, in a symbiotic relationship with them – were the vaudeville troupes, companies usually specialising in a variety of musical and theatrical routines. Not all groups worked to the same format but, taken as a whole, vaudeville programmes included items such as solo or group singing (usually with accompaniment), solo or group instrumental performances, tap dancing, mime, comedy, recitations, character impersonations, dramatic sketches, juggling and acrobatics. Historically, these vaudeville troupes were distant descendants of the minstrel tradition, but now they took their place alongside the bands in sharing the presentation of a genre of all-night entertainment known as 'Concert and Dance'. Like the bands, their repertoire was derived from both foreign and local sources, and like them, too, they produced cultural exemplars. The Palladiums or the Darktown Negroes in the 1910s, the African Darkies or the Versatile Seven in the 1920s, the Darktown Strutters, Harmony Kings, Pitch Black Follies and Synco Fans in the 1930s and 1940s: troupes such as these set standards, dictated trends and created role models.

Mbaqanga, Kwela and Other Styles: the Late 1940s and Beyond

So began a time of astonishing innovation: not only of South African swing; not only of *mbaqanga*; but somewhat later also of *kwela*, the extraordinary *marabi*-derived pennywhistle music of the streets, produced by the children of the black slums in creative imitation of their favourite jazzmen; and, no less remarkable, of the multitude of jazz-based vocal groups. These vocal groups, with names like the Manhattan Brothers, or the African Inkspots, began by doing superb imitations of American groups such as the Inkspots or the Mills Brothers, learnt precisely from recordings and translated into the vernacular. But soon they too produced their own original compositions, either in the American style or – more significantly – in a new, close-harmony township style based on *marabi*, or on the songs of migrant workers, or even on traditional songs.

The legislation of the 1950s, and the official violence that implemented it, put some of the final touches to the consolidation of the apartheid state. Most serious for the future of urban black music was the Group Areas Act of 1950, in consequence of which all remaining racially-mixed neighbourhoods were separated through the forced removal of entire black communities – often uprooted from the centres of cities and relocated on the peripheries. The destruction of these vibrant communities was a major factor in bringing the era of the large dance orchestras to an end, by the late 1950s. For a while, smaller groups survived. With as much energy as before, these smaller groups worked once again in two different directions. One direction – towards America – looked primarily to the virtuoso bebop style of Charlie Parker and Dizzy Gillespie; the other looked again towards the fertile indigenous soil of *marabi*. As had frequently happened in the past, both tendencies made efforts to overlap, to find points of convergence, to understand their importance to each other. Many exiled South African musicians who later came to enjoy major international reputations – such as Abdullah Ibrahim (Dollar Brand), Hugh Masekela and Jonas Gwangwa, or the late Chris McGregor, Dudu Pukwana and Johnny Dyani – served their apprenticeship here: in this era, and in this confluence.

1960 was a decisive year. It saw the unleashing of a period of unprecedented state repression and, politically and culturally, it was the end of an epoch. It is the year of the Sharpeville massacre, the outright banning of the major arms of the popular liberation movements, and police arrests on a massive scale. It is also the year in which the SABC established a divisive, ethnically based radio service for blacks, with seven full-time ethnic services whose musical bias was towards traditional, neo-traditional, and religious music; the record companies followed suit. In the new black townships, suitable performing venues were virtually non-existent.

And so the exodus of jazz musicians for Europe and the United States began; most never returned. Those who remained had to find some way of adapting to the new situation, but those who were unable to adapt simply packed away their instruments for ever. As if to symbolise the new musical order, Mahlathini – one of the new order's first commercial products – appeared in animal skins and sang of the virtues of tribal life. Music had become inextricably tied to ideology

It is important to understand that one of the reasons jazz was suppressed was that it aspired to (among other things) musical and social *equality*: it was precisely that musical idiom in which and through which urban blacks were proving to themselves and to the world that they were the equals of whites (without in the process abandoning valued aspects of their black culture, or of their history as blacks who were assuming aspects of western culture). At the very moment that the white and racist South African state was devising an ideology and a programme for fragmenting black South Africans, for turning them against each other by reinforcing and artificially cultivating ethnic and racial differences, black jazz musicians and audiences were insisting not only on their necessary unity as blacks and as South Africans, but also on their status as fully-fledged and equal members of the international society of human beings. By adopting jazz, urban black South Africans were proudly and self-consciously identifying themselves as actors on the international stage of world history.

But the identification went further. For jazz was not only international: at times it was also, and very significantly, a discourse aspiring to the status of an international musical vernacular of the oppressed. Moreover, it was a discourse with explicit and historic roots in the continent of Africa, and it had been cultivated by people of colour – by former Africans – in the United States, under conditions of explosive capitalist development. The parallels with South Africa were obvious.

For a genuine politics of opposition, as much as for a culture of resistance, the next two decades suffered the aftermath of massive defeat and a slow rebuilding. Musically, few artists managed to open up any creative space within the rigid, anodyne, formula-bound styles fostered by the SABC's black radio stations. Africans who remembered the previous era coined a term for the bouncy new popular music, massproduced by the studios with the help of able but guileless musicians from the countryside: derogatorily, they called it *msakazo* (broadcast).

Memory, History and Context

When a virile, popular oppositional culture finally began to reappear, it did so because of, and almost simultaneously with, the re-emergence – on a momentous scale – of black working-class and community politics. In 1983, a few months after the launch of the United Democratic Front (UDF), at an historic, sold-out concert, a big band of older African jazz musicians – many of whom had not played publicly for 20 years – gave their inaugural performance under the name of the African Jazz Pioneers. It was, as had been the inauguration of a mass resistance movement, a ritual of regeneration, the release of energies and processes stifled for two decades. Things did not look the same afterwards. The striving for an authentic South African culture gained a momentum which even an endemic State of Emergency was unable to still. *Isicathamiya* choirs and 1950s-style bands shared the stage with the speech-makers at huge Cosatu and UDF rallies. New performing venues, such as Kippies in Johannesburg, sprang up in the major cities: through these passed musical groups of breathtaking originality, offering syncretic styles of a range, depth and variety absent from the South African stage for decades.

Bands such as Sakhile, Bayete, Sabenza, and Johnny Clegg's Savuka – as well as countless others, many of them less well known – played music in which the blend might be *mbaqanga* with traditional Nguni song; Cape Coloured *klopse* idioms with bebop; *marabi* with electronic rock; Zulu guitar style with Cape Malay *ghommaliedjies*; or many other permutations. It is what these integrations discovered and made possible that was exciting and important, for, like their audiences, the bands were wholly non-racial, rejecting in their behaviour and commitment, centuries of racial and class dichotomy. Their music was an alchemy, helping, in its way, to corrode the old social order and to liberate the new.

One of this alchemy's most astonishing features was that its power was, and still is, felt beyond the frontiers of apartheid society – by countless thousands of music lovers across the world. It is not enough to say that the crowds who flocked to stadiums in London, Abidjan, Paris or New York to hear this music did so *simply* because they support the struggle for social justice in South Africa. The immediacy and intensity of their emotional response suggests rather that they have taken this music for their own, and that the struggle and the hope it signifies resonates with their own struggles and hopes.

Yet, lamentably, in South Africa today – in the situation of endemic violence that now grips the land – the musical euphoria of the years between the mid-1980s and the start of the 90s has waned. Those years of heady experimentation now begin to seem as though they might, after all, turn out to have been only an interregnum, rather than the onset of a period in which resurgent creative energies were unstoppable.

There were great musical achievements during this interregnum; but they could not have come to pass without the rich and complex musical heritage that preceded them, and certainly not without the momentous, if now unsung and forgotten, achievements of the period before 1945. It is to that era that we must now turn our full attention.

CONCERT AND DANCE

The Foundations of Black Jazz in South Africa Between the 1920s and the Early 1940s.

The explosive development of a jazz-band tradition in South African cities from the 1920s, closely allied to the equally rapid maturation of a vaudeville tradition – which had been in existence at least since the First World War – is one of the most astonishing features of urban black culture in the first half of the century. Surrounded by myriad other musics – styles forged by migrant workers; traditional styles transplanted from the countryside to the mines; petty-bourgeois choral song; music of the church and of western-classical provenance – jazz and vaudeville quickly established themselves as the music which represented and articulated the hopes and aspirations of the most deeply urbanised sectors of the African working class.

This did not happen without fierce controversy. Around, and indeed within, this generalised 'jazzing' subculture were played out the frequently contradictory and overlapping strategies and inclinations of urban blacks: at one moment conciliatory, at another oppositional; now conservative, then radical; rooted in the politics of petty-bourgeois assimilationism or in those of an increasingly militant working-class consciousness. Although one can discern the existence both of different class tendencies and different musical genres, the relationship between economic class and musical genre is not straightforward – competing classes might have supported the same genre, or one class might have identified with different, apparently contradictory, genres.

This complex state of affairs is not confined to music, but is one aspect of a more general problem in the relationship between class and culture in South Africa. Recent South African historiography has brought the problem to light. Summarising such findings, Marks and Rathbone, for instance, have argued that it is 'impossible to consider African working-class culture and consciousness as in any sense watertight or closed off from the rest of the black population'.[1] Bozzoli has concluded that '[w]hile there may be economic classes in the making in South Africa, there have been few 'class cultures'.[2] One reason for the difficulty of identifying class with culture would seem to lie in the sheer physical nature of the ghetto, the microcosm where 'classes get squashed together and lose their sharp edges of distinction' so that 'interests fluctuate'.[3] Another would seem to derive more specifically from the dialectics of racism where, because of 'the racial barriers to ... social progress and economic betterment', the black section of the petty bourgeoisie has often been impelled 'to align "downwards" and seek the political support of the black lower classes, emphasising a racial commonality'.[4]

Concert and Dance

The crucible in which black jazz developed in South Africa was the performing and participating convention known locally as 'Concert and Dance'. Typically, it belonged indoors and to the night. Hounded not only by the hated pass laws but also by night curfew regulations, and lacking adequate public transport, Africans living in the cities devised a variety of institutions capable of sustaining indoor entertainment throughout the night. 'In spite of the trials and tribulations, segregation, oppression and poverty', wrote Johannesburg arts columnist Walter Nhlapo in 1936, 'efforts are continually made to make life sweet and brilliant.'[5]

The most visible as well as the most lustrous of these efforts was the Concert and Dance – characteristically a vaudeville entertainment from 8 p.m. to midnight, followed immediately by a dance which ended at 4 a.m. (Figure 1) Through this institution – hosted as it was in venues ranging from ramshackle township halls to fashionable centres such as Johannesburg's Bantu Men's Social Centre (BMSC) or the Ritz Palais de

---

1 Shula Marks and Richard Rathbone (eds), *Industrialization and Social Change in South Africa*, Johannesburg, 1982, p2.
2 Belinda Bozzoli (ed), *Town and Countryside in the Transvaal*, Johannesburg, 1983, p40.
3 Tim Couzens, 'Nobody's Baby: Modikwe Kidobe and Alexandra 1942-6', in Belinda Bozzoli, *Labour, Townships and Protest*, Johannesburg, 1979, p99.
4 Kelwyn Sole, 'Black literature and performance: some notes on class and populism', South African Labour Bulletin, 9:8, July 1984, p55.
5 *Bantu World* [hereafter referred to as *BW*] 15 February 1936.

Dance – passed all of South Africa's greatest jazz and vaudeville artists. It was a crucible in which the two styles were seldom totally distinct; instead, despite some obvious differences, they fed off each other, at times in a quite symbiotic relationship. Edward Sililo, who played trumpet with the Jazz Maniacs – one of the country's legendary bands – during this period, recalled that the music of the troupes was 'very, very close' to that of the bands: not least 'because most of the songs they played, the bands were playing. They used to come to the bands to ask for the lyrics of the numbers, and then they'd sing these things'.[6]

In truth, there was often a *structural* connection between bands and vaudeville companies: a particular band might regularly appear on the same bill as a particular troupe, provide musical backing for certain parts of the troupe's programme, add additional – sometimes essential – members to the cast from their own ranks, and share the same management.[7]

Whence did this repertoire derive? Broadly, from two huge, complex source areas, one American the other local, which were absorbed into the repertoire in different ways and in different proportions. Of the two, the American source accounted for what was by far the larger share of the repertoire.

For several decades, urban Africans were held in thrall by American culture – but above all by the activities and achievements of blacks in that society. Where American culture fascinated, *black* American culture infatuated. The ways in which this infatuation was expressed, and the uses to which it was put, provide an illuminating insight into some of the psycho-social dynamics of Africans in South African cities during the 1920s, 1930s and early 1940s. Most obviously, the infatuation furnished inspiration: examples for imitation, standards to be striven for and exhor-

---

6 Author's interview: Edward Sililo, Johannesburg, 1 December 1986.
7 Many old performers stress this interdependence. The close connection between one of the top dance bands (the Merry Blackbirds) and one of the top vaudeville troupes (the Pitch Black Follies), for instance, has been pointed out by Marjorie Pretorius, among others. Starting around 1940, she was the Blackbirds' first vocalist – but they regularly shared the bill with the Follies, and then Marjorie (as well as instrumentalists from the band) would often appear as vaudeville artists in the Follies' shows. Or the band would provide instrumental backing. 'We were one thing with the Pitch Black Follies', she says. A year or two before she joined the Blackbirds, Marjorie had been vocalist for the Jazz Maniacs (also *their* first). At the same time she and two other women belonged to a small troupe called the Harlem Babies, who frequently appeared in the 'Concert' when the Maniacs provided music for the 'Dance'. Their routines, directed by comedian Petrus Qwabe, included singing, dancing and acting, and 'the Jazz Maniacs used to background us'. (Author's interview: Marjorie Pretorius, Johannesburg, 18 October 1987.)

Marabi Nights

tations to achievement. Invoking the example of 'black stars such as the late Florence Mills, Layton and Johnstone ... Paul Robeson and many others', and noting that many African children with 'a burning love of music' were 'struggling against the limitations imposed by poverty', a columnist for *Umteteli wa Bantu* offered these words of encouragement in 1930:

> *My opinion, based upon exceptionally intimate experience spread over some years, is that the musical talent of the Bantu is as pronounced as that of the American Negro. It is unfortunate that the Natives of South Africa are themselves unaware of their musical talent.*[8]

Such intimations were commonplace and insistent. Eleven years later Wilfred Sentso, famous vaudeville artist, jazz-band leader, composer and educationist, wrote in the same paper:

> *Today in the playing of musical instruments you find many Negroes on the top: Coleman Hawkins, Fats Waller, Duke Ellington and Paul Dunbar are but only a few of some outstanding Negro instrumentalists ... We can do it here too!*[9]

Indeed, in their own various and different ways, many artists were already attempting to do it here too. This was signalled on occasions such as when Pixley's Midnight Follies 'tried to imitate the American crooning twang', or the African Theatrical Syndicate 'with painted lips and faces smeared jet black, imitated Negro crooners'; when the Mercury Stars of Pretoria 'kept the audience cheerful with the latest stunts from America', or a crowd turned up to watch a demonstration of 'Susie Q. – latest dance craze – a Harlem creation!' to music provided by the much-admired Rhythm Kings Band under JCP Mavimbela; when the influential commentator Walter Nhlapo proclaimed himself to be among 'the followers of "le jazz hot"', or noted that the great blues and boogie-woogie pianist Sullivan Mphañlele had been 'an ardent admirer and imitator of the late Fats Waller'. At these and countless other moments, notice was being given that not merely individual performers or styles, but an entire subculture, were in the process of being emulated; and there was a hope that Johannesburg, or any other South African city for that matter, would

---

8 *Umteteli wa Bantu* [hereafter referred to as *UWB*] 25 January 1930. The author ('Musica') is very likely Mark Radebe. 'Musica' is, in any case, probably an early version of 'Musicus', a pen-name Radebe was using regularly by 1932.

9 *UWB* 18 January 1941. Paul Dunbar is the odd-man-out in this list: he was not an instrumentalist at all, but a poet and lyricist!

'one day develop a Harlem of its own which will compare with New York Harlem'.[10]

These exhortations and emulations were based on the confident assertion of a racial and cultural identity between blacks in South Africa and those in the United States. People of colour in the US – as an editorial in *Umteteli* insisted in 1932 – were 'Africans in America'; *therefore* their achievements were a source of very great encouragement to 'Africans in Africa'. Thus the 'soul-moving' vaudeville duo, Layton and Johnstone, though American, were in truth 'of African origin'. By a similar logic the classical composer Samuel Coleridge-Taylor, though he was born, lived and died in the south of England, was saluted as a 'West African composer'. Just as significant, it was 'a fact that the greatest American works of music, the works that will live, have been influenced chiefly by African melodies and rhythms'.[11]

If infatuation with the United States provided the inspiration and the examples, it also set the standards and furnished a *means* by which local artists could be deemed to have succeeded. Favourable comparison with an individual, group or style in the US was the ultimate stamp of approval. For the top performers, such accolades were common. Peter Rezant, leader of what many considered to be the country's most prestigious dance band, the Merry Blackbirds (Figure 2), remembers that he used to feel immense pride when audiences confirmed that they could detect 'no difference' between his band's performance of a number and the way that number sounded on an imported record.[12] Though their greatest rivals, the Jazz Maniacs (Figure 3), were less accomplished readers than the Merry Blackbirds and therefore often learnt pieces directly from recordings, that did not prevent them from achieving the same standards or receiving similar compliments. As Dale Quaker, himself a bandleader in the early forties, recalls:

> *For instance, you take a song like 'The Woodchopper's Ball'. You know, the way the Maniacs used to play that, it was exactly like the American bands used to play it. Type of fellows who could listen to a thing and then play it. And you wouldn't be able to make out the difference – whether they're playing from an orchestration or not. They were good at that type of thing.*[13]

---

10 *UWB* 14, 21 January 1939; *BW* 29 August 1942; *UWB* 4 September 1937, 1 January 1939, 3 April 1937, 22 January 1944.
11 *UWB* 29 October 1932; *Ilanga Lase Natal* [hereafter referred to as *ILN*] 9 September 1932; *UWB* 11 November 1933.
12 Author's interview: Peter Rezant, Riverlea, 3 June 1984.
13 Author's interview, Dale Quaker, 1986.

Indeed, Peter Rezant – though he speaks of his greatest rivals – is keen to remember assertions that the Jazz Maniacs played that number even *better* than the Americans:

> When they couldn't read off the score they would buy the record, and try and play all those difficult solos of the big professional men, like for instance Woody Herman's 'Woodchopper's Ball'. They play – like one white musician said to me one day, he says, 'You know the way I heard those fellas play "The Woodchopper's Ball", I would say that it sounded better than on the record!' – That's how they played, they played very well.[14]

Such attainments often left audiences incredulous. In 1936, when the Merry Blackbirds appeared with the Pitch Black Follies, the country's leading vaudeville troupe, at the British Empire Exhibition in Johannesburg, the reported response of the amazed crowd was to dismiss them, saying 'Agh, those are Negroes from America!'[15]

When it came to the handing out of accolades, comparisons were there in plentiful supply, each time doing duty as a kind of graduation certificate. In 1940, when a trio consisting of Solomon 'Zuluboy' Cele (Figure 4), leader of the Jazz Maniacs (on saxophone and clarinet), Wilfred Sentso, leader of the Synco Fans troupe (on piano) and Kenneth McBein, temporarily with the Jazz Maniacs (on drums), appeared with the Synco Schools troupe, Walter Nhlapo found this group similar to that of Louis Armstrong and the Lyn Murray Choristers (whose 1938 recording of four spirituals he presumably had in mind). A year later he compared the newly-formed Gay Gaeities to the Mills Brothers, and not long after announced that an ensemble of 'girls' within the Pitch Black Follies 'would be praised by the Peters Sisters, Duncan Sisters, Andrews Sisters and the King Sisters'. Around the same time, tap-dancing duo Jubilation and Nice – also members of the Pitch Black Follies – were hailed as the South African Nicholas Brothers, while the versatile Jubilation's guttural singing was described as 'Armstrongian' and hence seen as a local example of this 'most wonderful achievement of a voice'. Outstanding soloists included Pitch Black Follies and Synco Fans vocalist, Emily Kwenane, a veritable Bessie Smith 'if she would only turn a blues singer' (or a Teddy Grace if she wouldn't), and the wonderful Sullivan Mphahlele, who would 'challenge... and frighten every pianist with his fingers'. He played like Fats Waller, was known as 'Fats Waller', and even died on the same day as Fats Waller.[16]

---

14 Interview by Eddie Koch: Peter Rezant, Johannesburg, 22 June 1980.
15 *Drum* May 1956.
16 *BW* , 13 November 193321 September 1940, 4 October 1941;

American accolades were found even for the most eccentric performers. Toko Khampepe, leader of the Bantu Revue Follies and pianist extraordinary, had a way of playing that left critic Walter Nhlapo gasping, but in the end not even Toko's curious brilliance was found to be without black American precedent:

> I can't explain this except if I were taught Psychiatry or practise it. It is wonderful how he pounds the piano. As time marches on, charmed by the strains of music, for it is said 'music hath its charms', he becomes hotter and hotter; bangs the instrument, leaves his stool, knees on the ground, plays with his back towards the piano, sits on the keyboard and plays with his haunches. Such playing is seen in Harlem.[17]

But, as the earlier references to the likes of Woody Herman and the Andrews Sisters suggest, the category of black American musicians was not entirely rigid in the minds of black South Africans: white Americans occasionally slipped in, perhaps because they were – rightly or wrongly – identified with the music made by the 'Africans in America'. Indeed, alongside the strong, emotive category of 'Africans in America', the performance culture of black South Africans drew on another, looser category, a commercial pantheon, filled with images of the stars and styles of Western – mainly American – popular culture. These images, too, found their way into the practices of vaudeville and jazz, where they also served as examples to be copied and as criteria of success.

At least as early as 1930, the black press carried prominent advertisements in which lists of Zulu records on the Zonophone label nestled alongside those of 'Dixie Records' featuring performers such as Jimmy Rodgers, the Carter family, and the McCravy Brothers. The ubiquitous 'Waiting for a Train' featured prominently, and promised the ultimate in identification: 'You can feel like Jimmy Rodgers himself!'[18] That was a thrill which thousands sought, as Es'kia Mphahlele recalls in his autobiography: 'At Christmas-time Jeemee Roe-Jars (Jimmy Rodgers), then in fashion, yodelled plaintively from various parts of the village'[19]

By the late 1930s, individuals and groups vied for comparison with selected white American models. The Kimberley Amateur Entertainers boasted a tap dancer whom they called 'our Ginger Rogers', while the Pitch Black Follies of 1938 – giving themselves a yearly identification tag after the manner of, say, the Ziegfield Follies – offered audiences a

---

ILN 9 December 1944; BW 28 November 1942, 22 January 1944; UWB 22 January 1944.
17 BW 19 October 1940.
18 ILN 25 July 1930; UWB 22 November 1930.
19 Es'kia Mphahlele, *Down Second Avenue*, London, 1959, p22.

special treat in the shape of little Doris Shuping, 'the copper-coloured Shirley Temple'. Not to be outdone, the Masinya Kids proffered not one, but an entire troupe of 'darkie Shirley Temples'. Still more exotically, and revealing the extent of the infatuation with images derived from American movies, by 1941 the Follies were including scenes with names like 'Hawaii Calls', which 'took the "house" to those fabulous islands of the South Seas'.[20]

Minstrel Shows and Vaudeville

By the time Concert and Dance exploded among urban blacks in South Africa, the American connection already had a long history. The missionary presence, cultural and educational contacts and economic interests were the main conduits which transmitted American examples, and through which they were sought.

A practice of special importance was the minstrel show which, in South Africa as in the US, was one of the most important forebears of vaudeville. Minstrel shows were introduced into South Africa surprisingly early: the Christy Minstrels arrived in Cape Town in 1862, another American minstrel troupe landed in Durban in 1865, and blackface minstrelsy quickly became massively popular among white South African audiences.

Blacks were exposed to the genre from the start: by 1880, at least one African minstrel troupe was performing in Durban.[21] In the end, however, as far as jazz and vaudeville were concerned, the most immediately significant repositories were the printed sheets of ragtime songs – often indistinguishable from 'coon' songs, as minstrel songs were called in their final stage – other Tin Pan Alley songs, phonograph recordings and, later, films and published jazz arrangements. Some of these were available long before the Concert and Dance institution absorbed them and turned them to its own ends. By 1904, for instance, recordings and tonic-solfa versions of ragtime or 'coon' songs were not only being sold in trade stores, but songs of this kind were also being performed by black choral groups.[22] And when, by the 1920s, the gramophone had installed itself as a common feature in the homes of blacks living in the cities,

---

20 *UWB* 9 July, 20 August 1938; *BW* 18 March 1939, 1 November 1941.
21 For a fuller treatment of the early history of the minstrel show in South Africa, see Erlmann, *African Stars*, Chapter 2.
22 David Coplan, *The Urbanization of African Performing Arts in South Africa*, Ph.D. dissertation, Indiana University, 1980, p164; and David Coplan, 'The emergence of African working-class culture', in Marks and Rathbone, *Industrialization and Social Change in South Africa*, p371.

access to American performance culture (even if this culture was sometimes mediated via England) increased dramatically.[23]

Vaudeville artist Tommy ('China') Beusen was not yet in his teens when he began buying records with money earned as a caddie for white golfers in the mid-1920s. By the time he joined the Africans' Own Entertainers in 1929 at the age of 15 (a group that was then newly formed but would go on to great fame) he already had a considerable repertoire of songs, learned from recordings: numbers sung for example by Layton and Johnstone, or Bing Crosby, or popularised by Jack Hylton's Band. The youthful Entertainers were also to extend their repertoire and hone their craft by copying recordings. China remembers the status attached to any owner of a sizeable record collection:

> We were very, very, very fond of buying records. You could go anywhere you like in a location – there's always records. Some people play them in the yard, you know, under the grapevine. Sit there and play with their records. Boasting! You know, it's like it is now: everybody wants to buy a posh house, well furnished, and a shining Mercedes there. Ja, okay, you look at those things. When you start working and you try your best, you want to buy yourself a Mercedes too, or a house. But then it was the records! Everybody wanted... Ooh, I've heard that record! Man, I'm going to buy that record![24]

When local jazz musicians bought and copied records, they were unwittingly doing exactly what their American heroes traditionally had done. In Davenport, Iowa, in 1918, Bix Beiderbecke had a gramophone and used it to memorise solos by Nick La Rocca.[25] In Johannesburg in the early 1940s, future band leader Ntemi Piliso listened to recordings and tried to play exactly like Johnny Hodges.[26]

For those who could read, there was also the other option. In fact, for a bandleader like Peter Rezant – always proud of the reading skills of his Merry Blackbirds – it was better to hear the recorded version *after* the band had mastered the piece from the printed orchestration. And Edward Sililo, the first trumpeter with the Jazz Maniacs, remembers that in 1929 the fledgling Maniacs often learnt American and English jazz and dance pieces from what he calls the imported 'piano leaflets' or 'vocal scores'.[27] Similarly, Pitch Black Follies star Lindi Makhanya's early and

---

23 Tim Couzens, *The New African: A Study of the Life and Work of H.I.E. Dhlomo*, Johannesburg, 1985, p67.
24 Author's interview: Tommy Beusen, London, 28 April 1986.
25 Frank Tirro, *Jazz: A History*, London, 1979, p205.
26 Author's interview: Ntemi Piliso, Johannesburg, 26 July 1985.
27 Author's interview: Edward Sililo, Johannesburg, 1 December 1986.

formative encounters with ragtime and vaudeville music took place when her Aunt Elda brought printed songs to Lindi's home and sang them, accompanying herself on the 'baby grand'. Despite her father's stern objections to 'that type of thing', Lindi learnt several songs in this way. One was Irving Berlin's 'All Alone'.[28] Thus a song by one of the most gifted composers for the contemporary American vaudeville stage, written for Broadway in or around 1921, was sung about three years later by an eight-year-old African girl in the suburb of Sophiatown in western Johannesburg.

Black South Africans were watching films long before the invention of the sound movie in the late 1920s. In 1924 Sol Plaatje, writer and political spokesperson, brought back films from the US which he screened in various parts of the country. But even prior to this, American missionary Ray Phillips had been using films as a method of social control in mine compounds[29] – a precedent broadly adopted by such institutions as the BMSC, whose 1926 annual report mentioned the screening of 'special feature bioscope pictures', among other things, to show that it was 'playing an active part in shaping Native leisure-time activities, moulding Native character, and enlarging Native outlook'.[30]

By the 1930s, there were a number of commercial cinemas for blacks. Johannesburg, for example, had the Goldberg, West End, Good Hope, Osrins, Star, New Palace Theatre and others[31]; and in most of the townships free films were shown out of doors, even on cold winter nights. Despite controls and strict censorship, the movies had an impact difficult to overestimate. For jazz and vaudeville artists, films were an apparently infinite source of things to be emulated or developed: ideas, melodies, songs, routines, dance steps, styles of presentation, ways of dressing, ways of playing; and of course they also provided ways of estimating local achievement. Lindi Makhanya remembers that Johannes 'Koppie' Masoleng – formerly with the illustrious Darktown Strutters, but by the late 1930s a member and the coach of the Pitch Black Follies – used to encourage the Follies cast to see the Hollywood musicals:

> He liked us to go to musical shows. Ja, all musical shows. We'd go there – he'd take the cast, you know. To get an idea, you see, how we must perform. He used to like us to go a lot to Ginger

---

28 Author's interview (with Veit Erlmann): Lindi Makhanya, Soweto, 13 February 1987.
29 Couzens, *The New African*, p292
30 BMSC Annual Report, 1926 (AD843/B73.1: Department of Historical Papers, University of the Witwatersrand Library).
31 *BW* 15 February 1936, 3 June 1939.

Rogers' and Fred Astaire's shows. You see? To get the style of Fred Astaire and Ginger Rogers, you know.[32]

Some, like Walter Nhlapo, felt that the troupes should pay even more careful attention to the Hollywood musical. 'Why can't troupes present different items like film studios?', he asked. 'For instance, 20th Century Fox's 'Rose of Washington Square' can never be either like R.K.O.'s 'Dance Girl, Dance' or Metro-Goldwyn-Mayer's 'New Moon'.'[33] But for top bands like the Merry Blackbirds and their audiences, the musicals were the ultimate, and stunning, confirmation. When he thinks back to the reception of his band after the impact made by such films as *Sun Valley Serenade* and *Orchestra Wives* – both featuring the Glen Miller band – Peter Rezant's excitement and pride is even today as fresh as it must have been in the early 1940s:

> Oh my God, these fellows [in the Merry Blackbirds] were very, very able, very, very able! When this picture of Glen Miller came out, where the band played 'Chattanooga-Choo-Choo', we were right on top of the mountain at that time. Right on top! When that music came out, we played it – 'Blue Serenade' and all those serenades and so forth. But 'Chattanooga' was the big number, and 'In the Mood' was big... those were there the big numbers. So when the crowds would hear that, after the picture had been shown, oh, they would go mad, mad, mad, mad, mad! The police couldn't stop them away from the doors in the places outside Johannesburg where we would go to, when they hear that sound. They – they relate the sound to the picture now.[34]

And at exactly that time, one of these same films (*Orchestra Wives*) provided fundamental inspiration for a young pennywhistle player, not yet out of his teens, who was to develop into one of the most important composers and bandleaders of the 1950s – Ntemi Piliso:

> What actually inspired me was the demonstrations by the trombones, you know when they —. So I thought, That's wonderful – I think I'd like to do the same thing! Unfortunately I couldn't get the trombone. Ah, so this chap had a clarinet for me. I said, Well as long as it's an instrument – because I want to play an instrument! I took up the clarinet and started from scratch.[35]

---

32 Author's interview (with Veit Erlmann): Lindi Makhanya, Soweto, 13 February 1987.
33 *BW* 28 December 1940.
34 Author's interview: Peter Rezant, Riverlea, 23 June 1985.
35 Author's interview: Ntemi Piliso, Johannesburg, 24 January 1984.

In a context of infatuation with black American models, the discourse surrounding Concert and Dance accorded special attention to two of the imported genres: spirituals and, not surprisingly, jazz itself. Like the minstrel show, the spiritual was one of the major contributions of American music to South African music in the nineteenth century. Visiting black American jubilee singers, in keeping with contemporary trends in black minstrelsy in the US, included spirituals in the programmes they sang around the country, and thus left a legacy that reverberated deeply in the consciousness of Africans. The first jubilee groups visited in 1890; they were the Hampton Jubilee Singers and Orpheus McAdoo and the Virginia Jubilee Singers, and by the end of the decade they had between them returned several times and made numerous tours.

The mission churches (especially the African Methodist Episcopal Church) continued the process of popularising the spiritual; in a different way, so did the separatist churches. Enoch Mgijima's millenarian Israelite movement, for instance, 'used a hymn book blending Xhosa words and melody with spirituals taught them by Black American Baptist missionaries of the Church of God and Saints of Christ'.[36]

Given this recent history, it is not surprising that urban Africans infatuated with black America should have built spirituals into their vaudeville stage practices, and, from the beginning, accorded them a special place; nor that Reuben Caluza, the universally loved composer and choirmaster, on his way home from a period of study in the US, should – as late as 1936 – have declared that he had studied 'Negro Spirituals' during his stay and have announced that he hoped 'to be able to spread the knowledge of them in South Africa'.[37] In short, all Africans associated with vaudeville would have agreed with the critic for *Ilanga Lase Natal* who, in 1923, asserted that through spirituals

> there breathes hope and faith in the ultimate justice and brotherhood of man. The cadences of sorrow invariably turn to joy, and the message is ever manifest that... every man will be free.[38]

And for this reason, many would have argued, spirituals are 'doubtless... the finest pure music which has yet come out of America'.[39]

About what exactly 'jazz' was, there was – initially at least – less clarity. Certainly it was one of the topics of the day. 'The great popularity which 'Jazz' music has attained in this country and in Europe', an editorial in *Ilanga* reflected in 1920, 'has caused a great deal of discus-

---
36 Coplan, 'The emergence of African working-class culture', p371.
37 *BW* 21 March 1936.
38 *ILN* 2 November 1923.
39 *UWB* 29 October 1932.

sion to arise concerning its origin'.[40] A consensus soon emerged; and when it did it was held to be 'unquestionable' that this music which had spread 'like a flame throughout the world' had its roots in 'the Africans' strong sense of rhythm'. Jazz, one letter writer eventually insisted, was 'a modified and cultured form of our old Bantu music or dance, and... sensible people will keep pace with the changing times'.[41] Thus the terms of the discourse in which jazz was self-consciously accommodated, were the familiar ones of identity-in-difference: jazz had been developed in distant parts of the world but its developers – even though they might have been unaware of it – were in essence Africans 'Africans in America' who, under the impress of changed social and economic conditions, had transmuted their ancient cultural heritage and made it relevant to new circumstances. It was a compelling argument for doing likewise in South Africa.

Indigenous 'Roots'

American – and primarily black American – culture, then, provided the main source for the Concert and Dance repertoire. But at the same time, and more significantly for the development of an authentic South African jazz, the troupes and the bands made use of styles and elements whose origins lay on their very doorstep. The most obvious of these were various types of traditional music, which reached the Concert and Dance stages of the cities more explicitly in the work of the vaudeville companies than of the bands. That they did is paradoxical: it was after all these very troupes that, like the bands, were aspiring to emulate what they held to be the most sophisticated foreign acts. Certainly the format of these vaudeville programmes – with their encapsulated scenes, their roots in minstrel shows, their affinity to variety concerts – readily lent itself to the incorporation of the most disparate items. But this does not in itself explain why materials of traditional provenance should have been incorporated, even if on a limited scale, in the form of songs, dances, and 'scenes from traditional life'.

So why should the need to include such materials have arisen in the first place? The evidence available suggests three related reasons. First, traditional music was seen as a rich and important heritage and one that deserved to be preserved. Such a view was already widely held – at least among the educated petty bourgeoisie – by the time the elite South African Bantu Board of Music announced, in 1931, that one of its constitutional aims was 'to undertake research work into Bantu Music, and to collect for preservation, folksongs in their original form'.[42]

---

40 *ILN* 3 September 1920.
41 *UWB* 29 October 1932, 22 July 1939.

This 'folk music', one of its most articulate defenders, the university-educated critic Mark Radebe,[43] wrote around the same time, 'is our most treasured cultural inheritance'. What made it important, he suggested, was that these songs 'are intimately associated with Bantu history and lie very near the heart of the people. In this music there is a mass of characteristic material'.[44] Never wanting for influential spokespersons, this viewpoint also enjoyed support from no less a figure than Reuben Caluza. Placed in charge of music at Adams College in 1936, he is reported to have said that his principal aim in the job would be 'the preservation of Bantu traditional music', and that he hoped 'to make a collection of old instruments and to form something like a folk dance society which will use purely African percussion, reed and string instruments'.[45]

The second reason followed from the first: since this traditional heritage was so rich in significance, if it was kept alive it could lead to exciting creative possibilities in the present. 'The African musician and harmonist has his chance therefore', wrote the editors of *Umteteli* in 1933; 'the world is waiting'.[46] But it was Mark Radebe who expressed the drift of the argument most profoundly. For 'music to be truly national', he wrote in an article devoted to the topic, 'it must be based on the idiom of the people. Those most valuable achievements in musical history have been essentially national in spirit.' Thus if 'a distinctive Bantu music' were to emerge, it would have to be based on what he called 'the only real Bantu music, namely, its folk music'. If this occurred, it could be the foundation for 'a golden age of national Art'.[47]

The third reason also followed from the first, but to a somewhat different end. The traditional heritage needed to be preserved, not simply because it was rich in significance or because it could nourish and enliven creative enterprise, but for the sake of those not yet born who would otherwise know nothing about their roots. Daniel Marivate, singer, composer and teacher, captured the spirit of this view in a letter written in 1935:

> *We are passing at an age when things purely African are being replaced by things European. We who are between, that is,*

---

42 *Imvo Zabantusundu* 17 March 1931.
43 The claim that Mark Radebe was university educated is made by Herbert Dhlomo (*ILN* 16 August 1952). Indeed, Dhlomo says that Radebe was one of Professor P.R. Kirby's first African students of music at the University of the Witwatersrand.
44 *BW* 21 October 1933; *UWB* 9 July 1932.
45 *BW* 21 March 1936.
46 *UWB* 11 November 1933.
47 Mark Radebe, 'Bantu National Music', *UWB* 9 July 1932.

partly brought up against Native Background and partly peeping into European life and culture have great responsibility for our race. We may either allow all native life, art, music, language to be crushed and wiped out or preserve all the present ideas, customs, life, music and art for those that will be born at the time when there will be not uncivilised Bantu... I think the black man of the future will want to know what kind of people his ancestors were and what kind of life they were leading, and to be able to satisfy himself that he has really got a peep at the life of the old Bantu he must read the ideas that actually came from his Bantu predecessors.[48]

There was undoubtedly also a fourth reason, the basis of which has been sketched earlier. Though largely under the control of upwardly-aspirant, mission-educated blacks who constituted what has been called a 'repressed elite', the Concert and Dance institution catered to blacks of widely differing social, economic and educational backgrounds. Many of these people would still have retained meaningful links with rural communities, and therefore with varieties of traditional music. More important, all of them would have found themselves thrown together in urban ghettoes, confronting similar problems, and having to deal with the same spectre of racial capitalism. Out of this common experience of racial and economic oppression, blacks in the towns developed cultural practices which frequently expressed this commonality, tried to accommodate differences of background and interest, and thus often attempted to transcend some of the incipient contradictions of social class.

If traditional materials appeared in the repertoire of the vaudeville companies in fairly explicit fashion, it was left to the bands to make use of these elements in more mediated form. What the bands did – side by side with their appropriation of dance music from abroad – was to assimilate the musical styles developing in South Africa's slums and ghettoes since at least the First World War and that (despite certain regional differences) appear to have fallen generically under the term *marabi*.

In recent years, a considerable amount has been written about *marabi* – some of it not free of sheer conjecture or even mythology. Although part of this work has been useful, occasionally even pioneering, our knowledge of *marabi* is still inadequate, both in its details and in its foundations; for this to be remedied, rigorous and painstaking research is necessary. For our present purposes, what is essential to our understanding of *marabi* as the prehistory of South African jazz, is that

---

48 Letter to J.D. Rheinallt Jones, 4 November 1935 (AD843/B47: Department of Historical Papers, University of the Witwatersrand Library).

(in the words of jazzman and journalist Todd Matshikiza) it was 'the name given to the "hot", highly rhythmic repetitive single-themed dance tunes' of the period from the 1910s to the early 1930s; and that these tunes 'were largely the illiterate improvisations of the musicians of the day'.[49]

Essentially, *marabi* was the music of a *variety* of secular social occasions, which usually had in common not only the activity of dancing but also that of consuming alcohol. Perhaps the most famous of its venues were the *shebeens* (the illegal backroom or backyard liquor dens, where various kinds of homebrew were sold), and the weekend-long slumyard parties. Since it was an original style generated in and by the ghetto, the claim that it was, more than any other style, the music *of* the ghetto, is probably not unfounded. It was also primarily a keyboard, banjo or guitar style based on a cyclic harmonic pattern, much as the blues was: the basic *marabi* cycle, however, may be said to have stretched over four measures, with one measure for each of the following chords: I–IV–I$^6_4$–V. The cyclical nature of this style clearly derives from traditional sources: in traditional African musics, repeating harmonic patterns (sometimes called 'root progressions' or 'harmonic segments') are fundamental. Indeed, as ethnomusicologist Gerhard Kubik has pointed out, cyclicity has also become 'an important basis of nearly all neo-traditional music in sub-Saharan Africa'. Kubik names these cycles in neo-traditional music 'ostinato harmonic patterns', and argues that they give rise to 'short forms' (as opposed to song forms) – clearly another annotation for what Matshikiza had described as 'repetitive single-themed' tunes.[50] Thus from a structural and harmonic point of view, *marabi* is properly to be understood as a form of neo-traditional music.

The melodies superimposed on these endlessly repeating patterns sometimes became legendary; sometimes lyrics were invented as well, and in some instances the lyrics contained political commentary or protest. A significant proportion of these melodies also appear to have had traditional origins. Edward Sililo, who in the 1920s played *marabi* piano at Ma Jeremiah's *shebeen* in the slum area of Doornfontein in Johannesburg, identified these melodies as 'a mixture of Sotho music, Xhosa music, Zulu music' – or more specifically as a mixture of their ceremonial songs. But that was not all: frequently the tunes would be drawn from a familiar stock of African Christian hymns. In such a case, 'we'd just take a separate portion of the [hymn tune] and then jazz it up –

---

49 Todd Matshikiza, 'Twenty years of jazz', *Drum* December 1951.
50 Gerhard Kubik, *The Kachamba Brothers' Band: A Study of Neo-traditional Music in Malawi*, Zambian Papers, No 9, University of Zambia, 1974, pp23-4.

dance that music!'[51] Yet another source of melodies were the commercially popular tunes of the day:

> You see, ahh, for instance they would have a song like, in the early 1920s there were songs like '(Oh) Yes, We Have No Bananas'. And we'd take a snatch from that and put it in the marabi. And I play – any tune I play: now anything I remember I play it same time. As it just crosses my mind I play it, but I keep the same rhythm all the way.[52]

This, then, was the manner: cyclical repetitions of one melody or melodic fragment yielding eventually, perhaps, to a similar treatment of another melody or fragment, and perhaps then still others, each melody possibly from a different source. And in this manner 'you played with no stop – you could play for an hour-and-a-half without stopping'[53] Throughout, rhythmic accompaniment would be provided by a player shaking a tin filled with small stones. One standard pattern, as demonstrated by Sililo, is among the most basic and widespread drum patterns of traditional Nguni music.

Other styles also left their mark on the melodic and rhythmic structures of *marabi*: types of coloured-Afrikaans and white-Afrikaans dance music known as *tikkie-draai* and *vastrap*, as well as the *ghommaliedjies* of the Cape Malays. There appear also to have been varieties of *marabi* associated almost exclusively with certain groups of Xhosa- and Zulu-speakers. The Xhosa version, reputedly less polished than mainstream *marabi*[54], was named *tula n'divile*, after the words of a song first made popular by migrant workers in Durban in the late 1920s[55] while the Zulu version – really a kind of 'concert and *marabi* dance' developed by Zulu migrant workers in Johannesburg – was termed *ndunduma*, after the Zulu word for the minedumps that seemed to them to symbolise that city.[56]

---

51 Sililo cites the traditional Zulu ceremonial song, '*Entabeni siyagibela, entabeni siyehla*', and the Christian Zulu hymn, '*Amagugu*', as examples of traditional and Christian tunes that were adopted – and adapted – by *marabi* keyboard players.
52 Author's interview: Edward Sililo, Johannesburg, 1 December 1986.
53 Author's interview: Edward Sililo, Johannesburg, 1 December 1986.
54 Dan Twala, quoted in Coplan. *The Urbanization of African Performing Arts in South Africa*, p210.
55 Erlmann *African Stars*, p39
56 Coplan, *The Urbanization of African Performing Arts in South Africa*, p233.

Marabi Nights

Marabi and its close relatives, together with the vital, hedonistic subculture that supported them, have long disappeared. In their original form, none of these styles was ever recorded or, in their day, even written about, except in the most cursory and disdainful fashion. What little we know we owe to those who, long after the event, had something they were able to remember, and committed a recollection to paper, or lived until a much later time when historians were interested in recording their oral testimony. Thus, for instance, about 20 years after the waning of the *marabi* era, the remarkable poet, playwright and journalist Herbert Dhlomo left a richly evocative reminiscence of *ndunduma* – his 'educated' prejudices notwithstanding:

> *Ndunduma concerts were real refuse dump affairs, musically and morally. They were attended by degenerate young elements, the uninitiated newly-arrived country bumpkins and the morbidly curious. The people danced to the accompaniment of an organ and a most cacophonic 'orchestra' of small tins filled with pebbles. The atmosphere was obscene. For the first time in the history of Bantu entertainments liquor was introduced. The functions were like nightclubs of the lowest order.*
>
> *And yet what naturally talented players the ragtime and the ndunduma concerts had! Vampers (as they were called) who improvised many 'hot' original dance and singing numbers at the spur of the moment, and who play or accompany any piece after hearing the melody once, and did so in any key; fellows who played music not because it was fashionable, but because they were born musicians – helpless victims of a Muse that gave them fire which consumed them as they could not control it, nor knew nor cared what it was; men who, like tribal bards of old, created beauty they knew not and flung it back unrecorded to the elements which gave it birth.*[57]

And nearly half a century after *marabi's* twilight years, Wilson 'King Force' Silgee, who began playing saxophone with the Jazz Maniacs in the mid-1930s and later led the band, recalled something of what it felt like to attend a *marabi* party:

> *Marabi: that was the environment! It was either organ but mostly piano. You get there, you pay your ten cents. You get your scale*[58] *of whatever concoction there is, then you dance. It used to start from Friday night right through Sunday evening. You get tired, you go home, go and sleep, come back again: bob*

---

57 *ILN* 20 June 1953.
58 A drinking vessel, as well as a unit of measurement for drink.

a time, each time you get in. The piano and with the audience making a lot of noise. Trying to make some theme out of what is playing.[59]

The association of *marabi* with illegality, police raids, sex, and a desperately impoverished working class, large numbers of whom would at any one time have been unemployed, stigmatised it as evil and degrading in the eyes of those blacks whose notions of social advancement rested on an espousal of Christian middle-class values. Yet, though both the bands and their audiences included members of this group in significant numbers, the heterogeneous nature of black ghetto society meant that there were also strong pressures towards the *inclusion* of *marabi* in the bands' repertoires. Edward Sililo, in 1929 a member of the fledgling Jazz Maniacs, remembered that the group used to play *marabi* tunes, either by ear or (occasionally) in written-out arrangements. This practice continued long after the band expanded[60] Even band-members who grew up in homes that deeply disapproved of *marabi*, knew the style and its tunes well. Many would be able to say with Silgee – who grew up in such a home but used to watch and listen to *marabi* 'at the window' – 'It got itself infiltrated in me'.[61] Not even the prestigious Merry Blackbirds steered clear of *marabi*. Peter Rezant makes the point quite emphatically:

> *You couldn't avoid that at that time, you see. Everything had that twist into* marabi. *Because it was the* marabi *era... They were little ditties, you know, coming from the townships – ditties as you hear them. And somebody would be suggesting who'd been toying around with them, and then ultimately we play them as we hear them. One playing the melody and the others would fit in and so forth. Well, the trumpet and the alto [saxophone] were always the lead instruments. Then, if the trumpet plays in front, then the alto should find itself the, ahm, the harmony, to harmonise – and so did the trombone. And the correction would come, to correct our harmonies, from the piano. That's how we began, you know, before the orchestrations came in.*[62]

Training Grounds for Jazz

To play orchestrations, band members – or at least some of them – needed to be able to read; to play 'township ditties', they only needed to

---

59 Interview by Eddie Koch: Wilson Silgee, Johannesburg, 11 September 1979.
60 Author's interview: Edward Sililo, Johannesburg, 1 December 1986.
61 Interview by MEDU: Wilson Silgee, Gaborone, July 1986. *Rixaka* 3, 1986, pp19-21.
62 Author's interview: Peter Rezant, Riverlea, 23 June 1985.

be able to play by ear. But to do either, the primary requirement was an ability to play the instruments. Where did they learn? An important part of the answer is suggested in the ironic reflection that, in the early 1920s, at least two future members of the Jazz Maniacs could regularly have been found sitting attentively in church. One, young Wilson Silgee, would have been watching his father, a church minister, coach the brass band that accompanied the choir during Sunday services; the other, a slightly older Edward Sililo, would have been holding a trumpet and doing his best to play along in a similar band, conducted by one Joseph Mmutle in the Wesleyan Church in Western Native Township[63]

In short, the most important preliminary training ground for danceband musicians were the missions, their stations and schools, and the brass (and other) bands attached to them, as well as the Salvation Army. (For vaudeville entertainers, the mission-school and church choirs, together with their school concerts, played an equally formative role). (Figure 5)

It was the British and German missionaries who had first introduced brass bands into South Africa – for the glory of God, the advancement of 'civilisation', and the procurement of converts. The scale of this musical intervention was impressive, and before the end of the nineteenth century, mission stations in every province had brass bands with which to buttress their appeal.[64] Africans soon appropriated the idea for their own, rather different, purposes. The Tswana and the Pedi seem to have been the first to establish autonomous brass bands – doubtless partly because their own long tradition of pipe-ensemble performance provided a context which facilitated the adoption of the 'new' Western aerophones.

The earliest of such bands appeared, wearing uniforms, in the Transvaal in the 1880s, sponsored by traditional chiefs to symbolise their cultural and political aspirations in the colonial situation.[65] As the black locations in the cities grew, and Africans found themselves increasingly herded together as proletarians, these brass bands began to lose their separate tribal affiliations. Thus appeared, for instance, Modikwe's Band, named after its founder, who had received training in the Salvation Army Native Band in Johannesburg, but left to set up his own band in Rustenburg in 1911; and the Bloemfontein-based Mokgoro Band, founded by Jeremiah Nlatseng in 1908 and still going strong (indeed even touring)

---

[63] Interview by Tim Couzens: Wilson Silgee, Johannesburg, 15 March 1979; Author's interview: Edward Sililo, Johannesburg, 1 December 1986.

[64] David Coplan, 'Marabi culture: continuity and transformation in African music', *African Urban Studies* 6, Winter 1979-80, pp58-9; and Coplan, *The Urbanization of African Performing Arts in South Africa*, p186.

[65] Coplan, 'The emergence of African working-class culture', p368.

30 years later.[66] Significantly, some of the proletarian bands participated directly in early vaudeville entertainments.[67]

But whether these diverse groups now played *ad hoc* arrangements of traditional African melodies, or typical band music, or hymn-tune accompaniments for use in church, or even their own more secular versions of hymn tunes, did not essentially matter: what was important was that an institutional form (with striking similarities to the contemporaneous New Orleans marching bands!) was in place, and that it was to have profound implications for the growth of a dance- and jazz-band tradition in South Africa. Or rather, the fact that these diverse bands played a diversity of musics mattered only in this positive sense: that the *variety* of musics produced and reproduced by the brass bands were the first steps toward the assimilation, by Africans, of a variety of styles within a Western instrumental tradition, and in ways later to be developed both within the Concert and Dance format and in the evolution of local jazz itself.

Nor did it matter, from this particular perspective, that the brassband institution tended to be appropriated for differing ideological ends. The 'repressed elite' adopted it for the symbolism of its Christian, Eurocentric affiliations, and its usefulness as a means of social discipline; in these hands it was fostered by organisations such as the Transvaal African Eisteddfod in the early 1930s. Whites, after the missionaries, also continued to establish black brass bands, and for not dissimilar reasons. The Witwatersrand Native Labour Association in the late 1930s imported a white bandmaster to create and train a band to play to African workers on the gold mines and, later, African brass bands were set up by the Native Military Corps as part of the war effort.[68]

Towards the lower end of the class spectrum, brass bands proliferated as well – but served quite different goals, usually related broadly to community needs such as economic support and solidarity. Most common were the marching bands that drummed up support for the *stokvels*.[69] A report in *Bantu World* in 1932 described one such band:

> *Gaudily attired men and women in uniform parade the Western Native Township on Sundays. The men are dressed in blue-*

---

66 *UWB* 5 November 1938. For more on Modikwe's Band, see Coplan, *The Urbanization of African Performing Arts in South Africa*, p191.

67 Jeremiah Nlatseng's Mokgoro Band, for instance, played in such an entertainment in the Community Hall, Batho Location, Bloemfontein, in July, 1923. (UWB 21 July 1923.

68 *UWB* 22 July, 18 November 1939, 3 February 1943.

69 For a fuller discussion of the *stokvel*, see for instance Ellen Hellmann, *Rooiyard: A Sociological Survey of an Urban Native Slumyard*, Cape Town 1948, p43.

serge military coats, sparkling with brass buttons, and white creped caps; while women dress in black skirts and white blouses. Forming rows, men at the van, and women at the rear, they march two abreast.

The Stockvell Band as it is called has drummers and trumpeters who play the music, while the rest sing. So appealing is their music that many crowds are attracted. This diverts many people in the township.[70]

Many *stokvels* dealt in alcohol. Where this occurred, they became difficult to distinguish from the illegal drinking houses known as *shebeens*, run by women known as *shebeen* queens, or *skokiaan* queens, after the name of one of their potent brews. Brass bands sometimes also marched to solicit clients for these institutions, providing occasions for disparagement by more 'respectable' location dwellers. A letter in *Bantu World* in 1937 exemplifies a typical outburst:

As civilisation advances, backwardness, paganism is also busy creeping on to retard our steady progress. We were rather jubilant that Tulandivile and the like were almost dying out and yielding place to classical music. Now, instead of Musical Schools increasing, Brass Bands are forming up in the locations to play things worse than Tulandivile – to assist the Skokiaan Queens by canvassing for more customers. These Brass Bands roam from one location to another attracting some worthy people and children as they go. Such mobs are not only an obstruction to traffic, but really suicidal to the African public...

Many children who have glittering opportunities to make good take such interest in these Bands that they grow a wish that they would be players of these Bands in future rather than be Pathfinder-masters. This sort of thing creates more Marabis. These children would have become learned men of eminence, made good for their country and their people. What suicide – as I say![71]

From the point of view of the developing jazz tradition, however, such ideological contestation was less important than the existence of the brass band as an institutional form. On the one hand, a regular columnist in *Bantu World*, writing from Johannesburg's Eastern Township in 1941, could remark on 'the noises of brass bands turning hymns into jazz tunes... in tents, rooms and under sackings all over the location'.[72] On

---

70 *BW* 17 September 1932.
71 *BW* 29 May 1937.
72 *BW* 18 January 1941.

the other hand, *Umteteli* in 1943 could interview Sergeant-Major C.W. Hall, formerly of the Royal North Lancashire Regiment, but now training a Native Military Corps Brass Band, and report that:

> (M)ost of his musicians came to him 'raw'. Some of them still cannot read or write their names, but through his training they have learned to read orchestral scores. The sgt-major said that they spent five hours daily practising and had become so proficient that, if called upon to perform, they needed no rehearsing... Pointing to his No.1 trombone player, a smartly dressed Mosuto soldier, sgt-major Hall said that he mastered the trombone in six months... 'My men play any march I put in front of them', he added... In addition, sgt-major Hall has organised a six-piece dance orchestra from among the same instrumentalists.[73]

Alongside the plethora of brass bands, other forms of instrumental tuition also developed, some of them still linked to the work of the missions, some quite independent of it. Many musicians were basically self-taught, often with the aid of books called 'instrumental tutors' which could readily be purchased from music shops. This, of course, presupposed at least a smattering of formal schooling and an elementary level of literacy – certainly never to be taken for granted in a society in which school attendance for blacks was not compulsory, and in which poverty determined that black children try to earn an income as soon as possible. When he wanted to learn the trumpet, Edward Sililo bought a 'Lawrence Wright' trumpet tutor and taught himself; Wilson Silgee, as an adult, learnt the saxophone in the same manner. With few exceptions, the private teachers were whites and for most blacks their fees were 'prohibitive'.[74]

Despite these contradictions, the black press regaled its readers with the success stories of those few who – in ways it never adequately explained – had scaled the peaks of music education in 'white' terms. An early favourite was one Reuben E. Davis. He was described as:

---

72 *BW* 18 January 1941.
73 *UWB* 13 February 1943. Modikwe's Band – mentioned earlier – was one of the most famous of the brass bands; the Merry Blackbirds were one of the most famous of the dance bands. An anecdote that vividly illustrates the general point at issue here is the fact that among the saxophone players of the Merry Blackbirds sat one Mac Modikwe – son of none other that the founder and director of Modikwe's Band. Mac had learnt to play his first instrument, the French horn, as a member of his father's independent proletarian brass band. (Peter Rezant, verbal communication, 17 February 1988.)
74 *UWB* 18 March 1939.

a Native living at Maritzburg who has demonstrated that achievement can be surmounted when the will to do so is strong enough. Mr. Davis has obtained the musical degree of ATCL — a success denoting both high courage and high ability. He is a Venda, the son of slave parents, and speaks Afrikaans and English but no Native language. He teaches music and five of his pupils recently passed the Trinity College examination.[75]

In such a context, it is a striking fact that many members of the top jazz bands and troupes of the 1930s had received at least some tuition from white teachers — by private arrangement as well as through the mission schools — and continued to procure white tuition as the need arose. This tells us something about the mixed socio-economic background of these groups, and their complex class composition. Wilson Silgee of the Jazz Maniacs — a group often simplistically described as a *marabi* band — would, as a boy, not only have been found sitting in church while his father coached the congregation's brass band; he could also have been found, aged about ten, perched on a piano stool in the private studio of a Mrs. Manson, a white teacher in Marshall Street, Johannesburg.[76] The lessons continued for a year. Later, as a pupil at Adams College, he continued to study music. Jacob Moeketsi, the most famous of the Jazz Maniacs' pianists, not only had a mother who sang hymns in the family living room while his father accompanied her on the organ; he was also a boarder at Healdtown Institution where he took lessons in classical piano from a white lady teacher.[77]

It was perhaps this same woman who taught Sol Klaaste — vaudeville piano prodigy, boogie-woogie artist and, later, pianist for the Merry Blackbirds and numerous other groups — when he too attended Healdtown in the late 1930s, but it must be said that by then he had already been taught privately by a Miss Brenner, ATCL, a Mr. A.H. Ashworth, Mus.Bac., and others.[78] Two of the first women in South African jazz — Hope Khumalo, among the earliest of the Jazz Maniacs' pianists, and Marjorie Pretorius, the first vocalist with the Jazz Maniacs *and* with the Merry Blackbirds — had both studied classical piano with a Mr. Goldberg, a white teacher in Doornfontein, Johannesburg.

Though initially self-taught, Peter Rezant of the Merry Blackbirds went on to find a German violin teacher in Johannesburg, and then took saxophone lessons from a certain George Louter who played in a (white)

---

75 *UWB* 10 September 1932.
76 Interview by Tim Couzens: Wilson Silgee, Johannesburg, 15 March 1979.
77 Author's interview: Sam Maile, Johannesburg, 28 September 1985; 'Kippie's Memories', *Staffrider* November 1981.
78 *BW* 1 August 1936.

band of the South African Railways. Rezant remembers that one of the members of the Blackbirds had studied music at Adams College, while another had acquired 'advanced' theoretical knowledge from a German music teacher in Rustenburg.[79]

Phillip Mbanjwa, trombonist with the Blackbirds, publicly stated in January 1934 that the band had 'a distinguished European teacher who gives them lessons every week'.[80] (In the mid-1930s the Jazz Maniacs also enjoyed 'the guidance of a European friend once in a while'.)[81] Thus do the examples proliferate.

A similar picture emerges from a close look at the vaudeville companies. Highlights here might include the efforts made by Johanna Phahlane, the versatile and brilliant founder and leader of the (all-female) Merry Makers of Bloemfontein. Writing about the preparations for what was probably the group's first Transvaal tour in 1935, she recalled that she had

made all arrangements to have training courses in the National-Theatrical movements at the Bloemfontein Grand Hotel Plaza with the able assistance of Miss M. Easton and Lady Eileen Burchmore so as to be fit for Johannesburg and other towns on behalf of my own Bantu people.[82]

Getting ready to tour with a newly reorganised troupe in 1937, she again arranged for 'private lessons'. These included 'classes in music by Miss Joyce Mayhew of the Grand Theatre Hall and by Miss Grinter of Eason's Pupil Dancing School'.[83] Another instance would be the Pitch Black Follies. This troupe included performers who had studied their craft with white teachers (musician and conjurer Victor Mkize had been a pupil at Dauby's School of Magic in Cape Town, and Griffiths Motsieloa had studied elocution in England),[84] but their stage education at the hands of whites did not end there. The company was famous for its dance and tap routines, among other features; these were devised largely by Johannes 'Koppie' Masoleng who, according to former member Lindi

---

79 Interview by Tim Couzens: Peter Rezant, Johannesburg, 30 December 1974; author's interview: Peter Rezant, Riverlea, 3 June 1984.
80 *BW* 27 January 1934. For their appearance at the British Empire Exhibition in Johannesburg in 1936, the Merry Blackbirds were coached by English dance-band leader, Teddy Joyce, who had been brought out with his band to play at the Exhibition. (Author's interview: Peter Rezant, Riverlea, 3 June 1984).
81 *UWB* 18 March 1939
82 *BW* 15 February 1936.
83 *UWB* 11 December 1937.
84 *BW* 5 November 1938

Makhanya, used periodically to take advanced lessons from white tap-dance teachers, and pass on what he had learnt to the Follies cast.[85] And after the spate of early-1940s films featuring Carmen Miranda[86] had boosted the popularity of Latin-American music among black South African audiences, Motsieloa approached a (white) South African professional ballroom champion by the name of Teddy van Rensburg to coach three men and three women of the Follies cast in Latin-American steps. 'They did very well with that', Peter Rezant remembers.[87]

In many respects the Concert and Dance tradition was shaped by, and evolved in response to, the experience of racial and class oppression. The irony of the matter is that many of the skills that this dynamically growing tradition was creatively shaping for its own use, and that blacks were energetically seeking to acquire, were skills that were already 'owned', and could therefore be sold, on their own terms, by whites.

Established black teachers of music (or of the other performing arts) were virtually non-existent. From about the mid-1930s, a tiny handful of black teachers of note began to appear. Among them were Reuben Caluza, who took up his music post at Adams College on his return from the US in 1936; Merry Blackbirds pianist Mrs. Emily Motsieloa, who was running a piano studio in Alexandra Township by 1937 (and possibly earlier); and Mrs. Marie Dube, American-born wife of Frederick Dube (nephew of former ANC president, John Dube), who opened a small music school at the Methodist Institute in Grey Street, Durban, in 1938.[88]

Perhaps none realised the importance of the black challenge to white educational hegemony as forcefully as Wilfred Sentso, founder and leader of the Synco Fans troupe, and a jazz pianist and composer of some stature. As early as 1930, while a teacher at Wilberforce Normal Department, and struggling for recognition as a composer, he wrote to Dr A.B. Xuma, then a Johannesburg medical practitioner but later to become president of the ANC:

> *My aim as a boy has also been to develop the theatrical music of our people as a profession besides my interest in the educational development of my people... I would realise my dreams*

---

85 Author's interview (with Veit Erlmann): Lindi Makhanya, Soweto, 13 February 1987.
86 Among the earliest of these were *Down Argentine Way* (1940), *That Night in Rio* (1941), *Weekend in Havana* (1941), and *Springtime in the Rockies* (1942).
87 Author's interview: Peter Rezant, Riverlea, 23 June 1985.
88 *ILN* 30 May 1936; *UWB* 3 April 1937; *BW* 21 May 1938. See also Ray Phillips, *The Bantu in the City*, Lovedale, South Africa, n.d. pp298-9.

of a scientifically organised education of our Bantu people as well in Music.[89]

He had been a successful conductor of the famous Wilberforce Institute Singers and had for some years held the position of head of department when, in 1937, he resigned and moved to Johannesburg to set up his own school of performing arts.[90] What he was really thinking about, as Todd Matshikiza wrote many years later, was the idea of

forming the biggest academy of jazz music for non-Whites in South Africa... He had no accommodation and no instruments. He had no money to buy either. All he had was the enthusiasm of a fire-cracker.[91]

He set up a temporary 'school' in the Bantu Sports Club, with branches in Alexandra Township, Orlando and Pimville, and distributed circulars offering tuition in piano syncopation, voice culture, tap-dancing, typewriting and music theory.[92] By June 1938 he had found new, and permanent, premises at Mooki Memorial College in Orlando; according to the printed letterheads, this was the headquarters of 'The Wilfred Sentso School of Modern Piano Syncopation'.[93] Within a year the institution had built up a reputation for teaching 'classical music, jazz syncopation, saxophone and trumpet blowing'; soon 'crooning, tap dancing and ragging' were to be added to this list, as was the existence of 'a fine troupe of young artists'.[94]

The contribution of Sentso and his assistants to Concert and Dance subculture was remarkable. Five years after the school began, *Bantu World* ran a report which summarised its achievement:

This month June the Synco Schools will be five years old, and in those five years it has produced outstanding artists found in nearly every musical organisation in the Reef. Names like Mad-Joe (Broadway Stars), Marjorie Pretorius (Merry Blackbirds), Edward Manyosi (Minstrels), Jubilation, Emily Kwenane (Jazz Maniacs) etc., and instrumentalists like Maurice Sabi (African Rhythmers), Sherwood [Mackay] Davashe (Merry Mischiefs), Henry Mienaar, Sandy Ngamza etc., African Hellenics etc. are

---

89 A.B. Xuma Papers (AD843: Department of Historical Papers, University of the Witwatersrand Library).
90 *BW* 29 January 1938.
91 *Drum* June 1953.
92 *BW* 29 January 1938.
93 A.B. Xuma Papers (AD843: Department of Historical Papers, University of the Witwatersrand Library).
94 *UWB* 18 March 1939, 27 January 1940.

all names to be found in the schools' registers... [Besides these, there are also the] Synco Fans troupe and the Synco Beats Band, which have performed in European Night Clubs, theatres, halls, open-air Stadiums etc., the largest show of which was sponsored by the West Rand Consolidated Mines where a crowd of over six thousand people attended for a one night's concert. The schools have also pioneered and published popular music by publishing well known popular tunes like 'Boon-Town', 'Lady Mine', 'Tsaba-Baby-Tsaba' etc.

To commemorate this fifth anniversary, a play entitled 'Five Years Service', script, music and all by Wilfred Sentso, will be staged in the Orlando Communal Hall... [The] Synco Fans Troupe and Synco Beats Band will be used in the cast.[95]

Sentso's performing arts school was a model, but one that would not be emulated for a long time. The fact that it existed at all was due not simply to Sentso's 'fire-cracker' enthusiasm, but to the beginnings of an important change in South Africa's social and political climate. These beginnings bore, as the decade of the 1940s wore on, militant consequences that could scarcely have been foreseen by Sentso or any of his colleagues. And they carried implications for a political 'deepening' of the Concert and Dance tradition itself. This, however, is a theme to which we shall return in the next chapter

Brilliant New Jazz

If the Concert and Dance institution was the crucible in which the black South African jazz tradition was forged between the 1920s and the early 1940s, the elements drawn into that crucible were diverse and even contradictory; and the proportions in which they were invoked, like the relationships between them, were unstable and changing. At one moment, these elements reflected the cultural legacy of colonialism and the growth of racial capitalism visited upon black South Africans – as well as the durability of aspects of traditional culture which survived in rapidly changing circumstances. Yet, at another moment, these elements reflected not so much the way the African working class *suffered* the colonial legacy, as its efforts to creatively appropriate it – while at the same time incorporating elements of traditional culture as a source of resistance drawn from a shared history. In this struggle between the cultural hegemony of the oppressor and the counter-hegemony of the oppressed, a dynamic, and ultimately brilliant, new jazz was born.

---

95 *BW* 19 June 1943.

MUSIC AND EMANCIPATION

The Social Role of Black Jazz and Vaudeville in South Africa Between the 1920s and the Early 1940s

As the music culture of South Africa's black city-dwellers grew in breadth and sophistication in the 1920s, 1930s and 1940s, a great and important question took shape within it. What could this music accomplish socially? Or, as the question was more elaborately framed at the first conference of the South African Bantu Board of Music, held on 1 and 2 July 1929: How could 'this heavenly gift... best be used for the glory of God and the amelioration of our social and cultural conditions?'[1]

The answers differed – and perhaps nowhere more widely than within the vibrant and virile subculture of jazz and vaudeville fostered by the most urbanised sectors of the black working class. But the differences here are not mysterious. This nascent, jazzing subculture itself contained somewhat contradictory preoccupations with, on the one hand, styles of jazz and vaudeville derived from the United States and, on the other, musical and performance styles that had developed long ago in the South African countryside, or more recently in the towns.

Nor did these contradictory preoccupations stand alone: they were rooted in, and grew out of, notions of society and of social change that were themselves contradictory.

---

1 *Imvo Zabantsundu* 4 February 1930.

It is often in the very language of these deeper beliefs about society that the question about music's social role was answered. As this suggests, the answers often lie outside the music itself: in the discourses that surround it, and in the contexts of its performance. The moment at which the music's own content begins substantively to provide the answers, marks (as we shall see) the moment at which the music's own social role begins to be fundamentally redefined.

What then were these beliefs? And what were the corresponding views about a social role for music?

The Moral Appeal in the Liberal View

On the one side were a set of beliefs essentially liberal and individualistic in character. They reflected in microcosm, and were surely in part a consequence of, the basically petty-bourgeois outlook and practice of (in particular) the African National Congress for much of the period between the 1920s and the early 1940s. For workers and slum-dwellers, this was a time of relative passivity, the result – it is usually held – of the ANC's failure to create in the black communities a viable organisational presence which would link up with the lives and struggles of the urban working class. As a result, the oppositional activities of this class were guided by what Gramsci would have called a 'corporate' proletarian consciousness – one, that is, which attempts to 'define and seek to improve a position within a given order' (in contrast to a 'hegemonic' consciousness, which 'seeks to perform a transformative work over the whole range of society.')[2]

In particular, two broad assumptions about music's social role stand out here, both concerned with ways in which music might be an aid improvement within the given order. The first assumption is that the music performed by blacks could demonstrate to whites that blacks were *worthy* of better social, political and economic treatment: in short, it should seek to effect a *moral persuasion*. On the analogy that 'God helps those that help themselves' – the columnist 'Musica' opined in an article on 'The Native and Music' in *Umteteli wa Bantu* in 1930 – 'so will assistance come from either the State or elsewhere if we shew ourselves worthy'.[3]

More euphorically, conservative poet and critic B.W. Vilakazi asked the readers of *Ilanga Lase Natal* in 1933 to believe that '[m]usic will

---

[2] I derive these references to Gramsci from Eddie Koch's excellent essay, '"Without Visible Means of Subsistence": Slumyard Culture in Johannesburg 1918-1940', in Belinda Bozzoli, *Town and Countryside in the Transvaal*, pp151-175.

[3] UWB 25 January 1930.

induce men of wider aspect to open for us gateways to economic and political liberty'.[4]

The argument rested – as so often in the developing South African subculture of jazz and vaudeville – on a presumption about what had happened in the United States. Paul Robeson, Florence Mills, and Layton and Johnstone were familiar examples: the fate of these and other 'descendants of a race that has been under worse oppression', 'Musica' argued, proves that 'developing our music and singing to the white man will do much better than some of the methods adopted in solving the intricate Bantu problem in South Africa'.[5] And when Robeson himself promised to visit South Africa in 1935 (a visit that ultimately never took place), the argument was put with renewed force.

The achievement of men like Robeson, an article in *Bantu World* claimed, 'has exploded the theory that the black man is mentally not the equal of the white man'; it is this kind of demonstration, accomplished in Robeson's case through music, that will help deliver local Africans 'from the thraldom of European oligarchy'.[6]

At home, the musical scene abounded with groups, bands and individual performers who were embarked upon a similar demonstration, and whose huge and enthusiastic audiences hoped for a similar deliverance. Appropriately – given their assumption about the political efficacy of moral persuasion – their repertoire was overwhelmingly American, learnt from imported gramophone records, or sheet music, or American films.[7] The best of these local musicians made regular tours of the country, sometimes even venturing into neighbouring states. Among vaudeville groups, none was more famous in the early 1930s than the Darktown Strutters. Reporting on a countrywide tour that, by May 1932, was already nine months old, *Bantu World* noted that the Strutters could 'boast of being the only Bantu group who filled the Durban and Maritzburg town halls with an appreciative audience of Europeans, with turns that are supposed to be associated only with European talents'. Better still, they were then 'deluged with invitations for private appearances among the elite of Durban European society, not as "curios" but as "eye openers"'.[8]

Musical performance as an 'eye opener': the image is significant, indeed central, to this mythology of moral persuasion, and recurs in countless variations, permutations and associated analogies. Playing to

---

4 'African Music: Where is it?' *ILN* 10 February 1933.
5 *UWB* 25 January 1930.
6 *BW* 2 February 1935.
7 The sources of the jazz and vaudeville repertoire, and the methods by which it was appropriated, are discussed in the previous chapter.
8 *BW* 7 May 1932.

full houses during a visit to Bechuanaland in 1936, the Darktown Strutters were again 'both an education and an eye-opener'; this was because they had showed that, 'given the opportunity', Africans were 'capable of rising above the ordinary standard of things'.[9]

In like fashion the following year, the Johnnesburg-based Merry Blackbirds – already famous as one of the finest dance bands in the land – were an 'eye-opener' in Port Elizabeth and a 'revelation' in Bloemfontein.[10] (Figure 6)

On such occasions, what eyes were opened to was not only the performance of the music itself, but a host of associated skills. One of these was the ability of many of the bands to read staff notation and therefore to play from imported orchestrations. Louis Radebe Petersen, a meticulous observer of the local jazz and vaudeville scene since the 1920s, and once pianist for various groups, makes this point vividly:

> *They wanted to prove to the world, I say the world, even: if anybody came from America or London or anywhere, if they put the music sheet in front of them they could read it and do it... It's how they turned the world upside down.*[11]

Among vaudeville performances, one act celebrated for its eye-opening potential was that in which Griffiths Motsieloa, leader of the famous Pitch Black Follies, recited 'Old Mother Hubbard' in four different languages, one of which was an impeccable English. The Follies worked closely with the Merry Blackbirds, whose leader, Peter Rezant, still smoulders with enthusiasm and pride when he recalls the impression Motsieloa would make:

> *He had a little programme of his own, you know, reciting in Xhosa, Sotho, English and Afrikaans. A wonderfully good job! And ah, well, he lived long enough to get the praises of the man who thought he had got onto a wild horse, you know – Professor Jabavu, when Professor Jabavu heard him in 1937 at Fort Hare, when we went for our first tour. At the end of the concert he came to say to the audience, he says, 'Well, I'm glad that I've lived long enough and this man is still alive, because I criticised him when I heard he was going over to England to take up elocution. I said, what is he going to do with elocution, this poor African boy!' We were standing right behind him the two of us, and the back of us were the cast – the band and the choir, the Pitch Black Follies. He turns round and he says, 'Griffiths, I*

---

9 *UWB* 14 March 1936.
10 *UWB* 17 April 1937, 10 April 1937.
11 Author's interview: Louis Radebe Petersen, Johannesburg, 2 February 1984.

must now shake your hands and tender my apology for having questioned your intelligence in wanting to take elocution!' In front here we had the Bishop of the Anglican Church, Bishop Ferguson! He says, 'With due respect to everybody here, can anybody tell me that he could speak better English or have recited better English than Griffiths tonight? Now I'm challenging everybody, and I'm including the Bishop, with all due respect, all here English speaking – I know all of us, 99 percent, are English speaking here. Is there somebody here who could have found any flaw in this man's English tonight?[12]

If eyes were to be opened, it was obviously not a matter of indifference whose eyes they were. The bands and vaudeville companies played, of course, predominantly to black audiences, but the demonstration of worthiness had ultimately to take place before the eyes of whites. Opportunities for such demonstration were avidly taken up. In 1941, for instance, the Merry Blackbirds, the Jazz Maniacs, the Synco Down Beats Orchestra, and the Pitch Black Follies performed in Johannesburg for the Blue Lagoon Club, the Log Cabin Club, and the New Paradise Club – events that prompted critic Walter Nhlapo to note approvingly that 'these European night clubs are serving [as] a factor [leading] to a better South Africa. They are breaking slowly but surely the segregation barrier set up by dirty politics...'[13]

In July of the same year, the Pitch Black Follies made their way to Durban and the south coast of Natal – the holiday playground of white South Africans – for a tour of hotels during the height of the mid-year holiday season. Through this invasion – as *Umteteli* styled it – black art and talent would be 'carried right to the doors of European South Africa', and the Follies would have 'the opportunity to "educate" a not inconsiderable section of Europeans'.[14] And in November, the Follies and the Merry Blackbirds performed at a home in Parktown, one of Johannesburg's most select white suburbs.[15]

These occasions also served as tokens of acceptance, and as signs that headway was being made. Some tokens carried special weight, as on those rare occasions when the *white* press noticed, and made favourable comment about, a performance by a black group; or better (and rarer) still, when a white band played a composition by a black composer. In 1944, the two top white big bands in Johannesburg each gave such a performance – events almost certainly unprecedented at that time. The

---

[12] Author's interview: Peter Rezant, Riverlea, 23 June 1985.
[13] *BW* 6 December 1941.
[14] *UWB* 14 June 1941.
[15] *UWB* 22 November 1941.

favoured composer was one Henry ('Japie') Mokone: in March, Charles Berman and his Orchestra played his 'My Heart is Beating Every Hour For You', and in August, Roy Martin and his Orchestra gave a broadcast performance of his 'I'm Blue Without You'. *Bantu World* at once supplied the familiar moral interpretation. These events, it proclaimed, were 'ample evidence of the composer's untiring efforts to demonstrate the fact that Africans are gifted musicians, not only in the sphere of African classical music, but also in European Jazz Music'.[16]

Yet the real reflection on such tokens was made a month later, in *Ilanga Lase Natal*. Alluding to the success of the Follies in winning 'the hearts of their white audiences', influential critic Herbert Dhlomo reported what one white observer had said to a member of the cast ('You have done more for your people during these two weeks than many politicians have done for years'), and concluded: 'I maintain that Art can, is and will continue to, play a great part in solving our problems'.[17]

Fame and Fortune in the Liberal View

The first broad assumption about music's social role, then, rested on the belief that whites were racist oppressors because they were ignorant; through music, blacks could help educate their masters and so present a moral claim that the white ruling class would find irresistible. The second assumption was as liberal as the first but more unashamedly individualistic. Its appeal was not to morality but to economics, its logic not that whites would change the system, but that blacks could play the system. It promised not a better deal for all, but a road out of the ghetto for some. Music, it said, could make you rich and famous.

Early support for this view came from an eminent quarter. Benjamin Tyamzashe, the famous Xhosa-speaking choral composer, gave it his blessing at the celebrated 1929 conference of the South African Bantu Board of Music. Giving his mundane advice a spiritual touch by reminding his audience that music was 'a social as well as a spiritual necessity, as in heaven they have nothing else but music', he went on to declare that 'the race' possessed 'men and women in South African who could become millionaires'.[18] *Umteteli*, like other black newspapers, took up the theme on numerous occasions. In 1932, for instance, an editorial

---

16 *BW* 5 August 1944.
17 *ILN* 9 September 1944. Dhlomo was writing here under his 'Busy Bee' pseudonym. (For a comprehensive clarification of pen-names, see T. Couzens, 'Pseudonyms in Black South African Writing', *Research in African Literatures*, 6:2, (1975), pp.226-231.)
18 *Imvo Zabantsundu* 4 February 1930.

noted that 'it may be... that there are individuals today whose voices, unknown to them, may be worth fortunes: just as Robeson's'.[19]

Though there were not yet any South African Robesons making their fortunes, the local scene seemed pregnant with possibilities. The Natal composer Reuben Caluza, for instance, had gone to London in 1930 for a series of recordings for the local market (which included many of his ragtime-influenced choral works). The records sold well. And the black press did not omit to report that in 1933, while studying in the United States, Caluza sang (with a group of fellow students) for both the American and French presidents.[20]

Griffiths Motsieloa's two recording sorties to London in 1930 and 1931 – both of them also involving other black South African musicians – were other events that aroused similar interest; so that when, in 1932, Motsieloa gave up teaching for a full-time career on the stage, *Bantu World* saw this as a sign that '[t]he Bantu people are on the march'.[21] Again the language is revealing. If this was a march, it was – for those lucky enough to be on it – one headed upwards, towards greatness, on a route that led out of the slums and into town. In an interview more than 40 years later, former vaudeville singer Tommy ('China') Beusen, once a member of the esteemed Africans' Own Entertainers, recalled the excitement of that journey:

> *[We] used to broadcast. Live, live, live, live! That Saturday morning, everybody stayed glued to the radio. Ayi, ayi, ayi! African Entertainers are going to broadcast this morning! When we finish there and we come into town [they] say, 'Ayi, man! You chaps were great!'... Yes, we are, we are up there now! You see? We up there and we the talk of the town!*[22]

Yet on this road from real poverty to promised riches lay a treacherous contradiction: music might be autonomously produced, but it tended quickly to became ensnared in structures of reproduction that were exploitative, geared towards profit, and not owned or controlled by those who created the music in the first place. Many experienced this contradiction, but none articulated it as clearly as the remarkable Wilfred Sentso, vaudeville artist, jazz musician, troupe and band leader, composer and educationist. Focusing on the record companies – the institution through which the contradiction was felt most acutely – Sentso gave the typical example of a studio paying a group £4 4s. 0d. for

---

19 *UWB* 17 December 1932.
20 *ILN* 2 June 1933.
21 *BW* 9 April 1932.
22 Author's interview: Tommy Beusen, London, 28 April 1986.

a double-sided 78 r.p.m. record. That fee would also purchase all rights to the music. Sentso commented:

> [I]t is no exaggeration to say that there are music houses which do a large turnover in Bantu recorded music, while the artists themselves go starving... After all the songs are yours; the voices are yours; the work is yours. The firm only comes in to collect the profits! Why, I repeat, sell your songs, your voices, all for £4 4s 0d? Fats Waller gets £400.[23]

The solution, he concluded, was for blacks to create their own musicians' union (a task which, a few months later, he set about trying to do).[24] Without such a union, he argued, there would be no protection against exploitation, no chance of the musician earning 'a living wage', nor, by implication, any possibility of music's leading musicians out of the ghetto.

The assumption that music could make one rich and famous – could change the quality of one's life – had unusual resonance for one stratum of performers within the jazz and vaudeville subculture: women. Black women, remarkably, managed to establish an – albeit tentative – gender-based position.

These women, particularly those living and working in the cities, were the subject of relentless discussion debate about their 'proper' roles, as wives, as daughters, as parents, but above all as present or future 'mothers of the nation'. The patriarchal attitudes and conservative morality of this discussion – conducted *inter alia* through the black press, the schools, and the churches – stressed such things as the importance of Christian ethics, dignified behaviour at home and an exemplary social demeanour abroad, unblemishable fidelity, devotion to duty, and the virtues of a temperate life. Within the rigid and constricting confines of this discourse, there was little place for the 'sinful' and inherently 'corrupting' world of jazz, dance and the vaudeville stage.

Despite this – indeed, in outright contradiction of it – stood the secular discourse of a developing show business, which made direct appeals for the incorporation of women, in particular ways and as a special category of performer.

In this jazzing subculture, women could at one and the same time make money *and* be exploited for their novelty value and their sex appeal (though, to be sure, the domination of the bands and vaudeville troupes by men meant that women's earnings were largely dependent on the generosity of the male leaders or managers).

---

23 Article by Wilfred Sentso, *UWB* 18 January 1941.
24 *BW* 15 November 1941.

But there is a dialectic here. The entry of women as wage-earners onto the performing stage slowly opened up a space which *women themselves* could define and which consequently accorded them new respectability. Women performers now became worthy of emulation, and this allowed them to begin tentatively to undermine, or at least extend, the rigid conventions of socially acceptable roles and behaviour. For women, then, music could play a role that was at least potentially progressive. It could slowly challenge the stereotypes of oppressed womanhood, deliver a blow to male hegemony, and provide a limited basis for economic autonomy.

Women performers were largely to be found in vaudeville troupes. Although mixed-gender and men-only groups were predominant, by the mid-1930s troupes consisting only of women, and even managed by women, were not uncommon. Nothing in their names gave even a hint of the subtle dialectic at work within them, as a few random examples will suggest. The Madcaps were a Mafeking group; comprising four women and two men, they were founded in 1928 by a Mrs. S.M. Molema, described as 'an indefatigable sports enthusiast and social worker'.[25] The Movietone Cabaret Girls flourished in Bloemfontein around the mid-1930s under the leadership of a certain Miss Florence K. Nthatisi, about the same time that Mrs. L. Kgokong was managing her Raven Girls in Pretoria, and not long after Miss V.N. Plaatje had founded her Rhythm Girls in Kimberley.[26] The Pitch Black Follies of 1937 consisted of some men and '30 charming girls in a sparkling revue'; these women divided into smaller groups and took the stage with names such as The Broadway Babies, The Ginger Girls, The Harlem Crazy Steppers, and The Dangerous Blue Girls.[27] By 1941, the Follies were fielding The Smart Girls, 'a troupe of four juvenile girls, whose singing and blending is remarkable', and The Hot Sparks with Peggy Bhengu, 'the best girl tapper on the stage of dusky Johannesburg'.[28]

In the jazz field, the space for women was restricted – as was the case in the United States – essentially to two roles: vocalists and pianists. Earliest of the pianists was certainly the extraordinary Emily Motsieloa, the first pianist of the Merry Blackbirds (in 1930 when it was known as the Motsieloa Band) who held that chair for nearly two decades.[29] (She was, as it happens, also wife of Griffiths.) Hope Khumalo was pianist for the Jazz Maniacs (Figure 7) for a short period around 1939 or 1940,[30]

---

25 *BW* 21 May 1932.
26 *BW* 18 January 1936, 17 April 1937, 9 June 1934.
27 *BW* 30 October 1937.
28 *BW* 24 May 1941.
29 Author's interview: Peter Rezant, Riverlea, 3 June 1984.
30 Author's interview: Marjorie Pretorius, Johannesburg, 18 October 1987.

after which she seemed not to play jazz again. (She resurfaces in April 1941 as the 'able accompanist' for the Johannesburg African Choral Society's performance of excerpts from Handel's *Messiah*).[31] The first female jazz vocalist – indeed the first black jazz soloist of either sex – was Marjorie Pretorius, who fronted first the Jazz Maniacs and then the Merry Blackbirds between about 1938 and 1961.[32]

Inevitably it was the women in the more famous groups who elicited the more public comment. The all-male Darktown Strutters had a well-honed reputation when, in the mid-1930s, and after much debate, they took in a 23-year-old singer by the name of Babsy Oliphant. Soon thereafter they included her sister Eleanor, and Lindi Makhanya, a young singer who had recorded with both Caluza's group in London, and the Bantu Glee Singers at home.[33] 'Gossip Pen', *Umteteli*'s critic, commented:

> The Oliphant sisters, notably Babsy, are perhaps best known for their courage. They dared the notions of Bantu conservatism and defied all the conventions which bespoke a less active life for Bantu maidenhood. And they have been a success.[34]

Lindi Makhanya, too, was hailed as a trend-setter. For *Bantu World* she was 'about the only African Lady, specially of her age, who has enjoyed such an exciting experience in her career as a musician'.[35]

But surely no woman made greater impact, or demonstrated greater self-consciousness about the implications of her career, than the brilliant Johanna ('Giddy') Phahlane, leader and manager of the celebrated Bloemfontein troupe, the Merry Makers. A pseudonymous letter writer in *Bantu World*, in January 1936, made the point crisply. Indignant that other centres in the country had not yet produced a female vaudeville performer of Phahlane's calibre, the writer insisted that '[o]ur womenfolk have a national gift which if keenly developed would make them stars on the stage'.[36]

It was a point that Johanna Phahlane herself took up energetically, almost in the manner of a one-woman campaign. Between 1936 and

---

31 *BW* 26 April 1941.
32 Author's interview: Marjorie Pretorius, Johannesburg, 18 October 1987. I have been unable to find any corroboration for Henry Nxumalo's assertion that 'Miss Nomvila, and Dolly Matsabe... helped give birth to the African blues' (presumably while Griffiths Motsieloa was recording in London?): see his 'How African Music-Makers Made the First Gramophone Record', *Umlindi we Nyanga*, May 1949.
33 Author's interview: Babsy Oliphant, Johannesburg, 13 May 1987.
34 *UWB* 30 April 1938.
35 *BW* 5 June 1937.
36 *BW* 25 January 1936.

1938, she wrote an occasional column for *Bantu World*, using the penname 'Lady Porcupine'. This became one of her most important forums. Here she joined with the struggle of African women in general, and here she propagated her belief that music could play a significant role in this struggle. Writing in February 1936, for example, she again drew attention to the contradiction between, on the one hand, the abundance of musical talent among African women, and on the other, the virtual absence of women from leadership positions on the musical stage. 'Surely', she urged, 'I am not the only young woman in this direction. There are others yet unsung: Forward girls!!'[37]

She made similar appeals from the stage. In January 1937, for instance, after two performances at different venues in Port Elizabeth (occasions that struck at least some members of the audience as the 'most successful functions ever staged in Port Elizabeth', and in which she impressed as 'the best lady we've seen on the stage'), Phahlane gave a closing speech in which she 'challenged the Africans to stand up and use their talents'.[38] But perhaps her most incisive appeal was made in *Bantu World* in May 1936.

In an article entitled 'A Modern Woman Struggles for Freedom', she delivered the sort of needle-sharp arguments that must have left her male readers feeling quite stung, and that made her pen-name seem aptly chosen:

> *Most men have said in all ages: 'Woman is stupid; therefore do not waste time and money in educating her much'. Let me be frank. Nowadays women are up in arms against this system. I could point to a score of women who really struggle forward for freedom in practical affairs of life... You will realise that a modern woman refuses to spend her time in dressing only for the captivation of gentlemen, as some may think, but will struggle hard to earn her living in many ways as a nurse, teacher, singer, actress, dancer, cook, dress-maker, house-keeper, laundress etc. and is very much anxious to make men comprehend that she can do without them... Now why should she be debarred from serving any state as a maker of laws? Stand in a pulpit and preach? Be a principal of any high school according to her high qualifications? Be a leader for men to follow her? There is no logical answer to these questions... But every silly clown of a fellow begins to cackle when a cultured and capable woman claims the right to take part in the control of a municipality or state...*

---

37 *BW* 15 February 1936.
38 *BW* 6 February 1937.

> *Do not imagine, O man, that your long supremacy can endure forever. Give a modern woman chance and work together co-operatively. She also has the right to struggle for freedom. Women of the race we all have to march – Forward.*[39]

Organisational Links and the Radical View

In what I have called the liberal view, then, the social role of jazz and vaudeville was as an aid to improvement within the given order. At the same time there was another view, and another set of practices, which viewed this musical subculture as potentially playing a more challenging role, lending assistance to efforts that *tended* in the direction of more fundamental social change. I shall call this the radical view. As was the case with the liberal view, it is possible here to distinguish between two broad impulses. The first – and earlier – is the assumption that music's socio-political role was largely a question of its formal links to oppositional organisations; and, as a corollary, that issues such as the specific style, content or provenance of the music were of secondary, or even minimal, importance.

One organisation which saw the issue in that way was the Industrial and Commercial Workers' Union (ICU). Founded in 1919 as a trade union, it grew rapidly, and by the mid-1920s was essentially a black protest movement with support in many parts of Southern Africa. The ICU seems to have had a close and ongoing relationship with music. In 1927, for instance, the year it was at its zenith with a claimed membership of 100 000, the organisation was hiring jazz bands to play at fancy-dress balls and other events in the ICU-owned Workers' Hall in Johannesburg. The best known of these bands was a coloured group, the Merry Mascots.[40] And in the corresponding venue in Durban, the ICU Hall, the break-away Natal branch often played host to vaudeville troupes. Performing there in 1932, for example, were Dem Darkies (from Pretoria), the Blue Dams (from Durban), the Midnight Follies and the Dixie Rag Lads (both from Amanzimtoti), as well the Famous Broadway Entertainers, the Sunbeams, and the African Youngsters. The Darktown Strutters themselves performed there at least once (in 1936).[41]

---

39 *BW* 30 May 1936.
40 Veit Erlmann, 'Black Political Song in South Africa – Some Research Perspectives', in *Popular Music Perspectives 2: Papers from The Second International Conference On Popular Music Studies, Reggio Emilia, September 19-24, 1983* (IASPM), Göteborg, Exeter, Ottawa, Reggio Emilia, 1985, p199.
41 Veit Erlmann, 'Singing Brings Joy To the Distressed', paper given at the History Workshop, University of the Witwatersrand, 1-14 February, 1987, p23 (a revised version appears as Chapter 6 of Erlmann, *African Stars*); ICU

Music and Emancipation

The ICU frequently organised large meetings and rallies, at which 'The Red Flag' or the ICU Anthem would commonly be sung;[42] and perhaps no association between the union and the jazzing subculture is more suggestive than that in which, at one such rally in 1929, 4 000 demonstrators marched through the streets of Johannesburg behind the General Secretary, Clements Kadalie, a jazz band belting out — and presumably 'jamming' to the tune of — 'The Red Flag'.[43]

A.W.G. Champion, leader of the Natal ICU, seems to have had a special interest in music, and in developing the union's relationship to music. He was, for example, on the quay to meet Caluza and his Double Quartette when the ship bringing them back from their recording sessions in England docked at Cape Town harbour in December 1930; and later that month he organised a concert — at which an ICU choir sang — to welcome them back to Durban. The previous year he had been infuriated by the bad publicity the *Natal Mercury* gave to Durban's African dance halls as a result of a speech made by the Rev. F. Scogings, and wrote an irate letter to Scogings, promising a public rebuke but demanding to know first whether he had really referred to the halls as 'dubious haunts of terpsichorean and alcoholic bliss'.[44]

Champion shared this interest in music with at least two ANC presidents: Pixley ka Izaka Seme, president from 1930 to 1936, and Dr. A.B. Xuma, his successor. In the late 1930s Seme managed — and gave his name to — a group calling itself Pixley's Mid-Night Follies. Xuma, at the same time, was managing the musical activities of jazz-band and vaudeville troupe leader, Wilfred Sentso.[45]

Though it seems to have been the most musically active, the ICU was not the only organisation to form links with the jazz and vaudeville subculture. The Communist Party regularly held dances to raise funds. Before the late 1920s, the only bands able to provide music suitable for

---

handbills ('Isaziso'), Forman Papers, University of Cape Town Library, BC 581 (B22.7 to B22.11); *BW* 16 January 1937.
42 H. Bradford, '"A Taste of Freedom": Capitalist Development and Response to the ICU in the Transvaal Countryside', in Bozzoli, *Town and Countryside in the Transvaal*, p135.
43 Eddie Koch, *Doornfontein and its African Working Class, 1914 to 1935: A Study of Popular Culture in Johannesburg*, MA thesis, University of the Witwatersrand, 1983, p172.
44 See *ILN* 26 December 1930; Champion's letter is in the University of Cape Town Library, BC581 (A1.32).
45 See for instance the Minutes of the Executive Committee of the Bantu Men's Social Centre, Johannesburg, held on 10 November 1938 (South African Institute of Race Relations Records, Library of the Church of the Province of South Africa, University of the Witwatersrand, AD843/B73.1); and *BW* 29 January 1938.

ballroom dancing were those comprising white musicians, and so groups such as Edgar Adeler's Personal Orchestra were engaged.[46] But as soon as high-quality coloured groups appeared on the scene – slightly earlier than African bands – the Party hired them. Thus in 1928, the Party's newspaper, *The South African Worker*, advertised that Rayner's Big Six were to play at a Grand Carnival Dance in the African Hall in Johannesburg on 12 September.[47]

In later years, more famous groups followed, among them Sonny's Jazz Revellers (probably the most celebrated coloured band of all) and the Merry Blackbirds. Various black trade unions, and the ANC, were among other organisations that also called upon the bands and the vaudeville troupes. In 1940, for example, when they were at the peak of their influence and membership with some 21 unions, the Joint Committee of the Non-European Trade Unions engaged the Merry Blackbirds to play for a dance,[48] and the Harmony Kings band played for a function at which '[d]ancing was interspersed by speeches from popular trade unionists'.[49]

The African Mine Workers' Union was formed in 1941; the following year it held a grand event in the common Concert and Dance format, and asked two of the country's top groups to perform: the Synco Fans (Wilfred Sentso's vaudeville company) and the Jazz Maniacs.[50]

But in terms of sheer publicity, or of grandness of conception, none of these events matched the vaudeville production informally promoted by the ANC, and staged in Johannesburg and Bloemfontein on numerous occasions between June and December 1943. Written, produced and directed by Madie Hall Xuma, the American-born wife of the ANC president, Dr. A.B. Xuma, the production was billed as an 'American Negro Review'; its first title, *The Making of a People*, was changed within two months to *The Progress of a Race*. Its purpose was to raise funds for the ANC; the last two performances, in fact, coincided with the ANC's annual conference, and a meeting of the All-African Convention. Advance publicity gave a brief description:

> Come and see the slaves arrive from Africa and sold in America. See them work on their master's plantation. Watch them develop and sing the Negro Spirituals. Hear them plan their freedom.

---

46 See for instance the *The South African Worker* 23 July 1926, 24 September 1926.
47 *The South African Worker* 22 August 1928.
48 *BW* 31 August 1940.
49 *BW* 20 July 1940.
50 *BW* 21 November 1942.

Figure 1: This 1933 poster advertises a Concert and Dance featuring two of the leading ensembles of the time: the Merry Blackbirds (a dance band), and the Africans Own Entertainers (a vaudeville group).
Source: J Pim Papers, Department of Historical Papers, Library of the University of the Witwatersrand.

Figure 2: The Merry Blackbirds as they were in (probably) 1937 or 1938. From left to right: Enoch Matunjwa, Ike Shuping, Emily Motsieloa, Peter Rezant (leader), Mac Modikoe, Tommy Koza and Phillip Mbanjwa.
Source: Peter Rezant's personal collection.

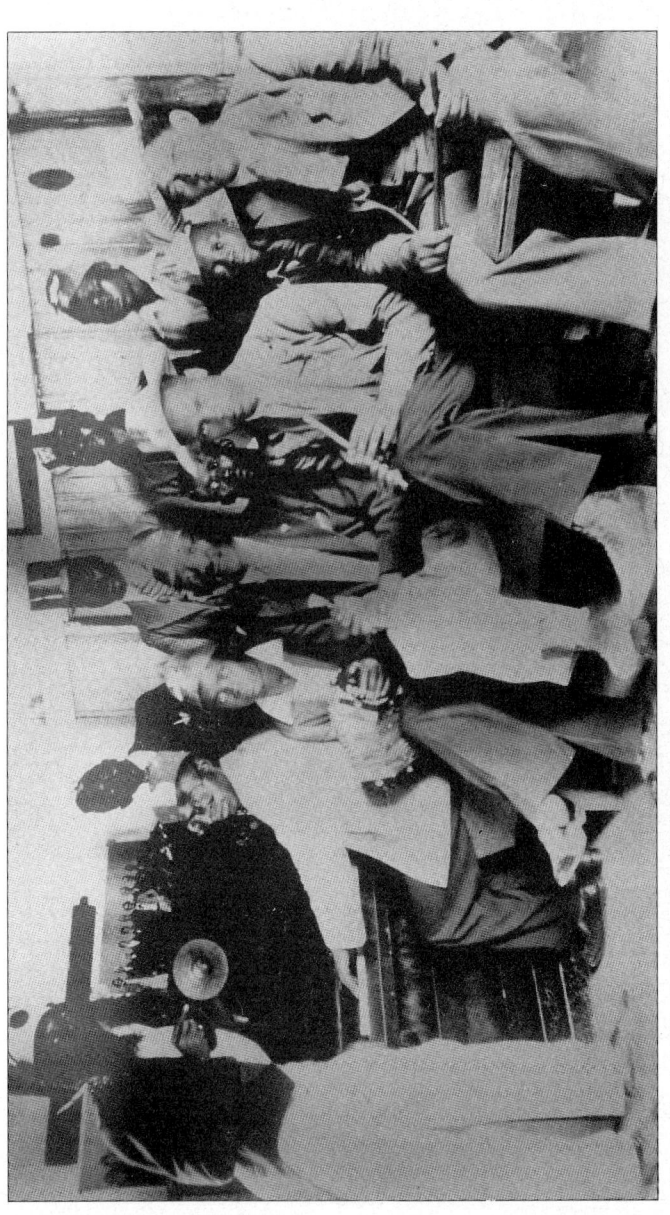

Figure 3: A 1931 photograph labelled 'our jazz band' – showing a group of instrumentalists from St Matthew's College, at St Matthew's Mission, Kieskammahoek, Cape Province. Peter Rezant, leader of the illustrious Merry Blackbirds, had himself been a pupil at this school in 1921 and 1922. *Source: Grant Collection, Library of the Church of the Province of South Africa, University of the Witwatersrand.*

Figure 4: Solomon 'Zuluboy' Cele, leader of the Jazz Maniacs, looking characteristically 'American'. The picture was taken around 1942.
Source: Mrs Solomon Cele's personal collection.

Figure 5: The Jazz Maniacs, in a photograph taken between 1934 and 1939. Jacob Moeketsi is at the piano; the leader, Solomon 'Zuluboy' Cele, sits in the front line, flanked by Wilson Silgee (left) and Zakes Nkosi. Behind (from the left) are Zakes Seabi, Vai Nkosi and Edward Sililo.

Figure 6: On tour with the Jazz Maniacs: a photograph taken in Cape Town in (probably) 1945. On the left is saxophonist and composer Wilson 'King Force' Silgee, who had recently taken over as bandleader after the murder of Solomon 'Zuluboy' Cele. On the right is Mackay Davashe, another of the band's saxophonists – he was later to become one of the giants of South African jazz. Between them is tap-dancer and Pitch Black Follies member, 'Nice' Molantoa who, with Jarvis Disimelo, made up the eminent tap-dance duo known as 'Jubilation and Nice'. In the early 1940s, the duo were regularly hailed as the local equivalent of the leading black American tap-dancers, the Nicholas Brothers.

Figure 7: Gallo's Singer label occupies an important niche in the history of South Africa's recording industry. Eric Gallo was 21 when, in 1926, he bought into Brunswick Records. Gallo and Brunswick were soon in stiff competition with both His Master's Voice and Columbia, the two British recording giants who dominated the South African market.

Initially Gallo sent its artists to London to record material for its new Singer Gramophone Company. But, after buying its own equipment in 1932, Singer's Johannesburg studio soon became the first permanent recording facility in sub-Saharan Africa.

The initial design for Singer's African recordings was ornate black and gold gilt. The paper sleeve featured a geometrical design in dark blue. The Art Deco-styled label and sleeve shown above was Singer's second design and dates from 1936. The drawings, in shades of light blue, suggest that contract mine labourers – a captive audience that craved entertainment and had a certain amount of disposable income – constituted a major component of the market for African records. For this reason, Singer's African catalogue emphasised the availability of recordings in a pan-tribal variety of languages and dialects. Other releases in the Singer repertoire, such as those by the Merry Blackbirds, appealed to the urban middle class. But there was one significant omission: the music of the slumyards was ignored, no doubt because the company regarded it as a poor commercial proposition.

Source: Rob Allingham

Figure 8: Sonny's Jazz Revellers (also known as the Jazz Revellers, or the Revellers Six), were certainly the most famous of the first generation of coloured dance bands. Founded in 1929, they were soon performing in major centres around the country. When this photograph appeared in *Bantu World* on 7 May 1932, the accompanying article noted:

Modern Ballroom Dancing, especially for the past few years, has become more popular than ever, and the standard of dancing among non-Europeans in this country has reached a very high level, and there is no doubt that it is largely due to the tireless efforts of this band, which has always made it a matter of duty to provide the very best musical fare.

(Those who sought a different sort of musical fare were less enthusiastic. For instance, as far as the Jazz Maniacs were concerned, 'We didn't like the way they were playing, because they were playing fast and all this so-called fox-trot.' Author's interview: Ernest 'Palm' Mochumi, Soweto 2 June 1984.)

Shown here (probably left to right) are Sid Meyer (conductor, pianist and composer), Stan Lambert (violinist and pianist), Johnnie Souris (singer and banjoist), Ike Augustus (tenor saxophonist), Sonny Groenewald (saxophonist and, for most of the band's life, its leader), and Chris Adams (manager and instrumentalist).

> *You will hear 'Old Man River' from 'Showboat' sung by an African 'Paul Robeson' double in music.*
>
> *After President Lincoln frees the slaves you will see the Negro develop and taking advantage of the newborn freedom under the 'Stars and Stripes' until you get in music Marion Anderson, world premier contralto, the versatile Paul Robeson, sometime scholar, sportsman, and great actor and singer; Hattie Macdaniels, Actress; Joe Louis – world heavyweight champion; Professor George Washington Carver, famous botanical and Industrial Chemist. All these characters and others will be impersoned.*[51]

The Merry Blackbirds provided instrumental backing, and played for the dance that followed.

If, through links of this kind, music was entering into oppositional political alignments, this happened for the most part behind the backs of the musicians themselves. With the exception of performers such as James Phillips – the coloured singer with the 'Paul Robeson' voice who frequently appeared with Sonny's Jazz Revellers and who was also a member of the Communist Party[52] – most musicians took a 'professional' attitude to such assignments. Merry Blackbirds leader, Peter Rezant, captured this attitude – and began to rationalise it – when he recalled his own band's work for the Communist Party:

> *I had no political leanings in any way. Anyway, I think that was also the success of the band. I didn't discuss politics with them – the only thing I was interested in was to entertain them... They were very highly cultured people. Their functions were on a very high plane, very high plane.*[53]

Rezant, then, though prepared to have his band provide music that gave functional support to the Communist Party, was not prepared to see his band espouse 'political leanings' that would have been detrimental to its 'success'. On any serious reckoning this is an artificial cleavage, but it would have found extensive support. When asked in a recent interview to comment on Griffiths Motsieloa's political attitudes, or those of his Pitch Black Follies, former star member of the group, Lindi Makhanya retorted: 'Oi, Motsieloa! He never wanted to be involved! (Laughs) Never! Ooh! He always wanted to be on the... good side of the law'.[54] But the

---
51 BW 5 June 1943. See also BW 14 August 1943; and UWB 5 June 1943, 19 June 1943, 4 December 1943, and 1 January 1944.
52 Author's interview: James Phillips, London, 8 April 1986.
53 Author's interview: Peter Rezant, Riverlea, 3 June 1984.
54 Author's interview: Lindi Makhanya, Soweto, 13 February 1987.

starkest of such disclaimers – and the one that provides the clearest statement of at least part of the underlying rationalisation – was made by John Mancoe in 1934, the same year that his *Bloemfontein Bantu and Coloured People's Directory* was published. In a letter in *Bantu World*, he proffered a spirited defence of Durban vaudeville celebrity, the 'great and famous musician and actor', Ndaba Majola:

> [H]is last show was nearly marred by reason of unfounded reports that he had clandestinely arranged to give financial backing to the activities of the Bloemfontein branch of the African National Congress in their agitation on domestic affairs of the location with the local authorities.
>
> As one who had assisted Majola in arranging his shows, I wish to refute and correct these misleading reports which would, if left unchallenged, place our Bantu Comedian in a most unenviable position, especially with our local authorities, when he pays Bloemfontein another visit in the near future.[55]

There were, however, occasions when musicians explicitly *chose* to identify themselves with a particular oppositional organisation or its work. A notable instance occurred less than a year after Mancoe's letter was written. Late in 1935, the Transvaal section of the ANC set out to raise funds to send delegates to the national meeting of the All-African Convention (summoned to protest about the infamous Herzog Bills which were to remove Africans from the common voters' role, set up separate political institutions for them, and fix for all time the unequal distribution of land).

Ten days before the meeting, scheduled for Bloemfontein on 16 December, a fund-raising dance took place in Johannesburg. The esteemed Rhythm Kings band, led by alto saxophonist John Mavimbela who had previously been with the Merry Blackbirds, considered the event sufficiently important to offer to provide the music free of charge. More than that: the band helped publicise the dance, the convention, the ANC, and the issues at stake. In a strongly-worded statement they explained their decision:

> We feel that it is our bounden duty and that of every true African to assist in every possible way those men who are going to Bloemfontein to consider the Government's Native policy, which in our opinion is detrimental to the future of our race. If there ever was a time when every man and woman of our race should stand shoulder to shoulder this is the time. The passing of the

---

[55] *BW* 29 September 1934.

Native Bills by Parliament will seal our doom and condemn us to perpetual servitude.[56]

These exceptions to the general 'professionalist' tendency took diverse forms. One thinks here of Merry Makers leader, Johanna Phahlane, who, writing as 'Lady Porcupine' in her column in *Bantu World*, sent from Bloemfontein an enthusiastic and supportive report on Kadalie's 'vigorous propaganda tour of the Free State' for the ICU;[57] and of William Mseleku, leader and manager of the famous Amanzimtoti Royal Entertainers, who was personally associated with the African trade union movement in the early 1940s, and who not long after became a committee member of the ANC's Natal branch.[58]

But for the vast majority of musicians who participated in events linked to particular political organisations, the naive cleavage between professional form and political function remained steadfastly unquestioned.

Politics in Music – Towards an African Style

In the first radical assumption, involving a more challenging social role for music, it is the links to organisations that were of primary – and virtually exclusive – importance. The politics, in a manner of speaking, was external to the music itself, so that political attitude *made no difference* to musical style. The second assumption, by contrast, draws these domains much more closely together. Here it is not simply a matter of organisations seeking to link music to their formal activities. Implicitly, a new demand is now made of music: that political stance *should affect* musical style, in such a way that the music itself comes to symbolise political character.

This shift – its outlines at first only dimly and intermittently perceived – ultimately had a profound and revolutionary impact on the future direction of black South African jazz culture. The shift involved the assertion that there was intrinsically a value in adopting or incorporating musical materials that were *African*. The precise nature of this value was never adequately spelt out by its advocates or practitioners, but there is no doubt that the belief was part of a broad groundswell that reached its first culmination in the early 1940s. Then, it inaugurated a period of militant protest; but it also – very significantly – found expression in the social and political philosophy of the New Africanism.[59]

---

56 *BW* 30 November 1935.
57 *BW* 13 June 1936.
58 Iain Edwards, *Umkhumbane Our Home. African Shantytown Society in Cato Manor Farm, 1946-1960*, Ph.D. thesis, University of Natal, 1989, p41.
59 For a full discussion of this philosophy, see Couzens, *The New African*.

One of those who helped give intellectual shape to this philosophy was the poet, playwright and journalist, Herbert Dhlomo. In an important essay written in 1949, he reviewed the failed strategies of the previous 100 years in terms that point to the need for a New Africanism:

> *During the period the African did not only admire, but envied and aspired to European ways of life. He thought education and proven ability would solve the question. He strove. He aspired. He was not content with his own [lot] as his fathers had been. He was even partly ashamed of his background, and tried to appease and win over the white man by appearing in the best light possible – according to so-called western standards. Rejected and frustrated, despite all his efforts, his admiration of the European turned to helpless envy and even to hostility. It was a phase in the long process of evolution.*[60]

The new, militant period which was taking shape in the early 1940s, was to stand in striking contrast to the lethargy of the preceding decade; yet it was in the relatively quiescent 1930s that its seeds germinated. The first tokens of the new mood of militancy became visible around the mid-1930s, occurring in response to the Hertzog Bills and other measures. On the one hand, the new legislation drove younger and more militant activists into leadership positions of the ANC and other organisations; on the other, these bodies – formerly petty-bourgeois in their outlook and cautious in their style – now began to perceive that all Africans were ultimately subject to a common fate.

The results of these changes are most clearly borne out by the ANC itself, which now entered a period of revitalisation and began slowly to change into a mass movement. In addition, the war produced a further set of factors which stimulated the growth of a more militant outlook. Wartime inflation and a huge flow of people from the countryside into the already crowded black city-slums added to the general level of grievance, while at the same time, the massive wartime expansion of the African working class led to a sudden surge in the trade union movement.

Symptoms of the new, militant mood were everywhere to be seen: in the location riots of 1937, 1942 and 1944, the police shootings of 1942, the bus boycotts of 1940, 1942, 1943 and 1944, and the huge squatter movements of the early 1940s. Politically, the momentum gathered during these years culminated in two signal developments: the forging of a deeper bond between the ANC and the Communist Party, and the found-

---

60 Cited in Couzens, *The New African*, pp273-4.

ing of the ANC Youth League in 1944 and its dramatic impact on the leadership of the ANC.

As with politics, so with music. The first signs of a shift in thinking about music also became apparent around the mid-1930s. A headline in *Bantu World* in February 1935 proclaimed it in summary form: 'Africans Must Not Ape Europeans'. The headline stood prominently above a major article written by Paul Robeson, and reprinted from the *Daily Herald*:

> *I am going back to my people... in the sense that for the rest of my life I am going to think and feel as an African – not as a white man... It is not as imitation Europeans, but as Africans, that we have a value...* [61]

Robeson was singled out as an important symbol, and example, of this early change in thinking: his intended visit to South Africa in 1935 provided occasion for a flurry of articles, editorials and letters in the black press. In February, for instance, a front-page article in *Bantu World* referred to Robeson's 'study of African music and life', and argued that his example should

> *reveal to our budding artists that there is sufficient material for their calling in the life of their own race, that there is drama, tragedy and comedy in the life of a people who are just emerging from the thraldom of Africa's darkness, and who are being rendered landless and homeless and exploited by an alien race in the land of their birth. This life can be dramatised.* [62]

In July, critic Walter Nhlapo took up some of these themes in the form of an impassioned plea:

> *One often wonders when Africans will learn to help, to be patriotic... We will rather sing the English National Anthem well and blunder with ours. What is wrong with us?... Was it not Paul Robeson who condemned the Negroes for trying to sing Brahms, Haydn, Wagner and disregarding their spirituals while Europeans singing them were amassing great fortunes?*
>
> *Again with African folk lore songs; we, like the Negroes, despise them and laugh and scorn at their singers.* [63]

Such appeals, to be sure, were part of a slowly changing cultural climate, and they were followed soon enough by audible and visible evidence of this change on the Concert and Dance stages of the country. *Umteteli*'s critic, Godfrey Kuzwayo, was one of the first to draw attention to it.

---

61 *BW* 16 February 1935.
62 *BW* 2 February 1935.
63 *BW* 13 July 1935.

Writing as 'Gossip Pen', the pen-name he used for his regular column, he declared in June 1936 that he had been struck by a new tendency in the productions of vaudeville companies. In the past, these productions had had a strongly 'European flavour' – but, he said, 'there has been a noticeable change in this regard, and concerts and dramatic shows are now being put forward with more and more African background in them'. To illustrate, he cited a forthcoming presentation by the Africans' Own Entertainers which was to include 'an African dramatic love tragedy', 'an Abakweta Ceremony', and 'a Zulu Witchcraft Dance'.[64]

It is important not to confuse this new tendency to create what one might call an African vaudeville, with the apparently similar – but differently motivated – ethnic vaudeville that had, for some four or five years, already enjoyed considerable success in Natal. The ideological underpinnings of Mtethwa's Lucky Stars and William Mseleku's Amanzimtoti Royal Entertainers – to mention the most famous of these Natal troupes – lay in what Erlmann has described as 'the gradual shift of liberal positions and urban reform projects towards an acceptance of territorial segregation and the idea of African reserves as viable repositories of black development'. Citing the work of Paul Rich, he attributes this shift to 'an ideological alliance' in Natal, which 'exerted a strong influence on African thinking about ethnic tradition'.[65]

Other kinds of music evidently lagged behind. In July 1936, Kuzwayo referred to the hundreds of Western-style African choirs in existence, and reiterated the widespread criticism that 'few, if any, have made any serious attempt to show their interpretative ability of real African music'.[66]

By the late 1930s and early 1940s, the clearest embodiment of the new African tendency was to be found in the work of a troupe calling itself the Bantu Revue Follies. Their programmes included 'sketches, drama, comedy and satire, also sentimental songs, jazz, madrigals and ditties – all of them in the Native vernacular'. The experience was of 'a real native concert' – the goal, clearly, of the troupe's leader, the extraordinary Toko Khampepe, who 'in loincloth and skins only, was a rare spectacle on the piano'. They were 'premier native music specialists and primitive artists'; it was they, more than perhaps any other group, who 'succeeded in reducing the commonplace in Bantu life to a fine art'.[67]

Some troupes sought to give expression to an 'African' repertoire in less sensational ways. For the Synco Fans, like their stable-companions, the Synco Down Beats Orchestra, this meant a resolve 'to play songs

---

64 *UWB* 13 June 1936.
65 Erlmann, *African Stars*, pp76-77.
66 *UWB* 11 July 1936.
67 *UWB* 23 September 1939, 22 March 1941, 5 April 1941.

composed and orchestrated by Africans'.[68] So too for the newly-formed African Minstrels, who preceded their launch in early 1941 with an announcement of the repertoire they would specialise in. They gave a list of eight categories including 'exclusive novelty numbers', 'musical comedies', 'old classical jazz songs', 'all-round minstrel choruses', 'operatic minstrel choruses', 'vaudeville revues', and 'specialities' – but at the top of the list stood 'African numbers composed by Africans'.[69]

No-one doubted that these changes were significant. Yet for some, the testy Walter Nhlapo among them, they still did not go far enough. Spurred on, perhaps, by the sharply rising political temperature of the early 1940s, he made bold in 1941 to point precisely to the social and political experiences of Africans that ought to be making an impact on the content and form of vaudeville productions. It was, quite simply, a call for 'committed' art:

> *The theatre of life is so full of incidents which when joined together would form a masterpiece sketch, but because most of these conductors are less imaginative and compositive but merely plagiarists, they fail.*
>
> *We have, for instance, the drama of pick-ups, the life in the zoo-like locations, the hooliganism and the like, subjects which are full of passion, of sorrow, of strife. We have scores upon scores of daily acts that deserve dramatisation but are passed over.*[70]

If for the vaudeville troupes, then, the Africanist impulse might be realised by 'not aping the Europeans', by 'presenting the commonplace in Bantu life', by staging 'songs composed and orchestrated by Africans', or by selecting 'subjects which are full of passion, of sorrow, of strife', what – under the sway of the same impulse – were the jazz bands to do?

Certainly, they too could play numbers composed by Africans, and band- and vaudeville-leader Wilfred Sentso was one of those to pursue this option with particular energy. As Todd Matshikiza was to recall many years later, 'Sentso began composing. Swing fever had touched him but he wouldn't touch imported music. He wrote his own numbers'.[71] Furthermore, in the composition of such numbers, jazzmen could find new ways to avoid 'aping the Europeans'. More positively, they could ignore conservative prejudice and instead celebrate and encourage local proletarian music-and-dance styles. Sentso and other composers did precisely this in the early 1940s for the popular *tsaba-tsaba*, a dance that

---

68 *UWB* 27 September 1941.
69 *BW* 11 January 1941.
70 *BW* 22 February 1941.
71 *Drum* July 1957.

was a successor to the notorious *marabi* dance. Open – let alone enthusiastic – support by a major critic for such a practice would have been unthinkable a few years earlier; but in 1941, Walter Nhlapo lent it his full weight:

> The origin of the indigenous Tsaba-Tsaba dance, which a year ago was the craze of Bantudom, is shrouded in considerable obscurity. Its originator is unknown and may never be known... One thing certain is, it first came to life at Sophiatown... In bioscopes we've seen Harlem dance the Big Apple, The Shag and Africa's creation, La Conga, and we've admired these creations, and these dances have not been recipients of abuse as Tsaba-Tsaba... If Tsaba-Tsaba is condemnable so is every dance... Tsaba-Tsaba is dusky South Africa's own creation art. Whether it is a fiend or not, it is an indispensable part of our musical and dance culture... There [was] no radio to broadcast it all over; but everybody sang it. There were no printed copies of it but some dance bands played it; it had the Spirit of Africa in it; the Life that's Africa, thus it inspired composers like Wilfred Sentso to give us the sensational 'Tsaba-Tsaba Baby'... Tsaba-Tsaba was a vogue even in the city's most polished and distinguished halls, but as is the lot of many popular dances, on introduction it was chastised as indecent, scurrilous and lewd.[72]

Alternatively, the jazz bands could give a richly African flavour to their renditions of American swing numbers by finding ways to incorporate elements of the harmonic and rhythmic structure of *marabi*. The Jazz Maniacs were one of the bands able to do this, perhaps partly because they were less adept 'readers' than, say, the Merry Blackbirds, and were therefore in any case less tied to the printed orchestrations. Former Maniacs trumpeter, Ernest 'Palm' Mochumi – himself once a *marabi* pianist – remembers that the band would still play the American charts 'straight'; but that 'when we played American music mixed with *marabi* style, [the audiences] used to be crazy over it'.[73]

But the most fundamental identification of jazz with the Africanist impulse was yet to come. Between the early and mid-1940s, a number of bands began experimenting with the interaction of a set of musical components now being brought together for the first time. The most readily identifiable were the cyclical harmonic structure of *marabi*, a slow, heavy beat probably derived from the traditional (and basically Zulu) secular dance-style known as *indlamu*, and forms and instrumentation adapted from American swing. With these was combined a languorous

---
72 *BW* 12 July 1941.
73 Author's interview: Ernest 'Palm' Mohumi, Soweto, 2 June 1984.

and syncretic melodic style owing less to the contours of American jazz melody than to those of neo-traditional South African music. The result was nothing less than a new kind of jazz: its practitioners and supporters were eventually to call it African Jazz, or *mbaqanga*.[74]

Mbaqanga had been on the agenda since at least 1941, the year in which Walter Nhlapo expressed the hope that the bands 'would play folklores in swing tempo'. 'After all', he declared, '[o]ur folklores are jazzy in tempo, and only require one thing: arranging the brutish rhythm.[75] Paradoxically it was this 'brutish rhythm' that became one of the defining characteristics of the new style. In an interview not long ago, Doc Bikitsha, an eminent critic and lifelong observer of the jazz and vaudeville scene, summed this up acutely.[76] In the early 1940s, he said, many black bands – among them the newly-formed Harlem Swingsters as well as the veteran Jazz Maniacs – started playing in what he termed an African stomp style:

> We call it African stomp because there was this heavy beat... There's more of the beat of Africa in it... the heavy beat of the African, the Zulu traditional...'

The rhythm of this stomp, as he demonstrated it, is immediately recognisable as the typical *indlamu* rhythm:

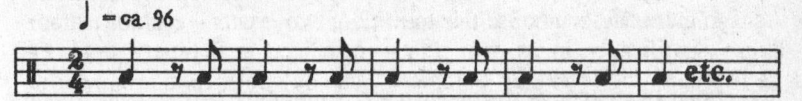

But it was former jazz pianist and composer, the late Todd Matshikiza, who in 1957 left the most evocative description of the new style. For him, what was of supreme importance was that this music represented the regeneration of *marabi*, the keyboard or guitar style of the slumyards, that (by the early 1940s) had been on the wane for at least 10 years. Todd claimed to have been party to its rebirth in a new form. A tour by the Harlem Swingsters had led them to the small Transvaal town of Potchefstroom. There, in this citadel of white Afrikanerdom, ironically

> African Jazz was reborn. The original product – Marabi – had died when American swing took over. Gray [Mbau], Taai [Shomang], Gwigwi [Mrwebi], and I recaptured the wonderful mood over an elevating early breakfast of corn bread and black

---

74 The term *mbaqanga* – commonly the Zulu word for a stiff, mielie-based porridge – has designated different kinds of music during the course of the last 40-odd years; but its first musical usage was as a synonym for African Jazz.
75 *BW* 22 November 1941.
76 Author's interview: Doc Bikitsha, Johannesburg, 24 November, 1986.

tea in the open air after a heavy drinking bout the previous evening. Gray put the corn bread aside and started blowing something on the five tone scale. We dropped our corn bread and got stuck into Gray's mood. And that is how some of the greatest and unsurpassed African Jazz classics were born. 'E-Qonce', 'E-Mtata', 'Majuba', 'Fish and Chips' were born out of that combination of the Harlem Swingsters whose passing remains today's greatest regret.

We invented 'Majuba' jazz [as the style was called in a later variant] and gave jive strong competition. We syncopated and displaced accents and gave endless variety to our 'native' rhythms. We were longing for the days of the Marabi piano, vital and live. Blues piano, ragtime piano, jazz band piano, swing and modern piano had taken it away from us. And here now we were seedling it again with new blood in its veins. It was [legendary marabi keyboard player] Tebejana's original material, but treated freshly with a dash of lime.[77]

The explicit and conscious acceptance of aspects of a social and political philosophy – in this case New Africanism – into the very constitution of music, was a turning-point in the history of black South African jazz. Musically as much as socially, the early 1940s was a time of transition. As if to mark and symbolise this transition, two events – each of extraordinary significance in its own right – coincided in February 1944. On 13 February, the legendary Solomon 'Zuluboy' Cele, former *marabi* pianist, and founder and leader of the Jazz Maniacs, was murdered in mysterious circumstances, and his body placed across the railway tracks at Nancefield Station in Soweto. Nine days later, on 24 February, and at a venue not far away, 12 people signed an attendance sheet as they gathered for a small but important meeting. The sheet is headed 'A.N.C. Youth League', and the occasion its inaugural meeting; among the signatories are Nelson Mandela, Oliver Tambo, Walter Sisulu, Anton Lembede, and Jordan Ngubane.[78]

'Zuluboy' Cele was one of the greatest of the first generation of black South African jazz musicians and band-leaders. The ANC Youth League was the political manifestation of New Africanism, the philosophy that had already begun to have a powerful impact on the jazz and vaudeville subculture, and on how it understood its social role. The coincidence of these events signals, for black South African music, both the end of one era and the beginning of the next.

---

77 *Drum* August 1957.
78 The Champion Papers, Library of the Church of the Province of South Africa, University of the Witwatersrand, A922.

MUSIC AND REPRESSION

Race, Class and Gender in Black South African Jazz Culture up to the Early 1940s

What the residents of Vrededorp saw and heard on Sunday, 21 March 1932, was a familiar event: a brass band parading through the streets of a South African city slum, playing a motley collection of *marabi* tunes, jazzed-up hymns and other popular melodies. The large crowd of excited participants who gathered in its train and brought traffic to a standstill knew very well that the purpose of the march was to drum up support for a *stokvel* – an informal savings society whose members held parties and contributed sums of money to each other in rotation. More to the point, perhaps, the crowd also knew that once they arrived at the party, chances were good that a potent, but illegal, home-brew would be sold.

But this particular Sunday the march never reached its destination. The police arrived, confronted the band and demanded that the music stop forthwith. ('Not that their music was bad', said the police.) Evidently fortified by the high spirits of the occasion, the band refused to stop playing, and all 18 members were arrested on the spot. Undeterred, they continued to play until they reached the police station – at which point the police summarily relieved them of their instruments, reminded them that they had been warned a fortnight earlier 'not to kick up a row in the streets, and cause crowds to collect', and fined each musician ten shillings. The record also shows that the police 'further deposed that every member of the band was somewhat alcoholic'.[1]

What is not recorded, is whether anything in this incident struck the band – surely as it must strike any reader today – as in the least surprising. Presumably, had anyone bothered to ask them, the members of the band would have pointed out that official interference in the music-making activities of black ghetto dwellers – like the resistance it met this Sunday afternoon – was a perfectly normal occurrence. For the environment in which South African jazz, and its parent and associated styles, grew up, was a society deeply hostile to its development, seeking to stifle it in a variety of ways. These hostilities cluster into two broadly differentiated categories: external repression on the basis of race, and internal repression based on class and gender.

External repression: Race

The first broad category of repression derived from forces which were largely *external* to blacks living in the cities, were imposed from above, and struck at the autonomy of certain of their cultural forms and institutions, leading to a struggle with white authority over performance *space*, *time* and *content*. More concretely: the black working class's creation of musical styles that symbolically expressed their urban circumstances, entailed a number of ongoing and interrelated battles – over venues, over the timing and duration of musical events, and over the very nature of these events.

Though these issues had a profound impact upon music making, they were, to be sure, part of a much larger set of social and political conflicts. 'Social life', Paul Claval notes, 'is inscribed in space and time';[2] and this is nowhere more clearly demonstrated than in South Africa where, as Bonner and Lodge have written, in the towns since the early twentieth century 'the policy of segregation has made the contestation of space one of the central political struggles'.[3]

Some of the conflicts around black performance were *formal*, the direct consequence of either legislation or *ad hoc* decree. Between about 1915 and 1935, perhaps the most important terrain for such contestation was the set of interlocking cultural institutions and practices broadly subsumed under the term *marabi*. These included, for example, the *marabi* party itself, its more exclusively regional or ethnic variants such as (Zulu) *ndunduma* and (Xhosa) *tula n'divile*, the *shebeen* and – particu-

---

1 *UWB* 26 March 1932.
2 Paul Claval, *Espace et Pouvoir* Paris, 1978, p1.
3 Philip Bonner and Tom Lodge, 'Introduction', in P. Bonner, I. Hofmeyr, D. James and T. Lodge (eds.), *Holding Their Ground: Class, Locality and Culture in 19th and 20th Century South Africa* (History Workshop 4), Johannesburg, 1989, p2.

larly when associated with the sale of illicit liquor – the *stokvel*. All were notoriously subject to continuous police harassment.

Since music – or 'noise' to those antipathetic to the events – was involved, these gatherings were easily discovered; and when nothing more incriminating could be found, the police used 'noise' as a pretext for terminating them. '[T]he police used to come there just to stop the noise', recalled Ernest 'Palm' Mochumi, former *marabi* pianist and jazz trumpeter. 'They just come and rush ... sjambok you out of the room. Then we run away ... jump through the window. Everybody – plus the owner of the house!' Of course, there would normally have been alcohol; and 'if they find it, then we're all arrested'.[4] And such raids were stepped up by the 1930s, when the police, by their own admission, began 'an incessant, relentless war' against the liquor brewers.[5]

So marked was the repression involved here, that it provided a topic not only for the members of the subculture directly affected by it, but also for more elite entertainers, who tried to stand aloof from *marabi*, but whose multi-class audiences would certainly have included people with direct experience of police raids. Even a dance band as illustrious as the Merry Blackbirds recorded a song on the topic, with lyrics sung by a vocal group, the Alexandrians:

Nank' amaphoyisa –
azosibopha.
Asbophel' ugologo.

Here are the policemen –
they are going to arrest us.
They will arrest us for [possessing] alcohol.[6]

Marabi culture had evolved in particular localities in response to specific material conditions; and damaging and disruptive though such raids were, they did not fundamentally alter the nature of the slumyards. Defensive and resilient from the beginning, *marabi* culture survived, and so, with it, did the innovative musicians whose polyglot creations were laying the foundations for a South African jazz tradition. But this was soon to change.

---

4   Interview by Deborah James and others: Ernest Mochumi, Johannesburg, date unknown.
5   Paul la Hausse, *Brewers, Beerhalls and Boycotts: A History of Liquor in South Africa*, Johannesburg, 1988, p44.
6   The Alexandrians with the Merry Blackbirds: 'Arayi Amaphoyisa' (78 r.p.m. 'Test Record', archive of the International Library of African Music, Rhodes University: never commercially released).

In the wake of the Urban Areas Act of 1923, officials began to lay claim to inner-city suburbs as 'white'; and as the 'repatriation' and then relocation of black residents began, so too did the definitive destruction of *marabi* culture commence. And most visibly so in Johannesburg: what began, in 1924 and 1925, as the ordering of 6 000 Africans out of the city, culminated in 1933 with the proclamation of all but three areas as white.

In fact, the removals delivered a terminal blow even before they were complete. Peter Rezant, leader of the Merry Blackbirds, recalls that when Africans were removed and 'Prospect Township died, then all those *shebeens* were killed'. Though blacks still lived in Doornfontein, the yards and *shebeens* in that suburb were not conducive to *marabi* performance; they were simply too vulnerable to police investigation. 'You see now, any noise would attract the police ... because the police were closer [than for instance in Prospect Township], and it's in town.'[7]

Nor were there any real opportunities for *marabi* musicians in the new black township to the south-west of Johannesburg in which blacks were resettled. With 18 000 people living in nearly 3 000 houses in Orlando by 1935, the township could in principle have supported a lively *marabi* musical culture, but a number of municipal regulations made this impossible. Perhaps the most repressive of these was a restriction issued by the Orlando Advisory Board, which in 1933 resolved that 'all night entertainments be not allowed in private houses – that is, entertainments that are conducted for money – by reason of disorder, rowdiness and being a nuisance to neighbours'.[8]

Marabi musicians soon realised that their art, stripped of the small, informal, domestic space which had nurtured it, had no future in the sterile new dormitory suburbs. Essentially *marabi* was a keyboard art; but the size and ambiance of the new township community halls, along with other factors (such as the near-impossibility of selling home-brewed liquor), ruled these halls out as viable alternative venues. Like other *marabi* musicians, 'Palm' Mochumi, the *marabi* pianist, now found himself without opportunities to play. Unlike most, 'Palm' had access to a trumpet, which he took up and so began readying himself for his next career as a jazz trumpeter.[9]

Even more 'respectable' city venues, never part of the *marabi* orbit, had their share of official harassment. In September 1923, for instance,

---

7   Interview by Tim Couzens and Julian Burgess: Peter Rezant, Riverlea, 30 December 1974.
8   Cited in Koch, *Doornfontein and its African Working Class, 1914-1935*, p230.
9   Cited in Koch, *Doornfontein and its African Working Class, 1914-1935*, p230.

the popular and well-supported Africans' Club in Johannesburg, applied to the Town Council's Public Entertainment Court for a dancing-hall licence. Despite the club's credentials – its 'respectability had not previously been questioned', it was controlled by a 'joint committee of Europeans and Natives' and its chairman and general manager, D.S. Letanke, also held high office in the Transvaal Native Congress – the application was opposed by the police and white property owners in the area, and the bid for the licence failed. As so often in the contestation of space, time and content in the making of popular culture in South Africa, argument about 'noise' furnished one (but not the only) pretext.

The court heard that

> the club premises were used by rowdy Natives, and that many young Native girls attended dances which began at 9 o'clock on Saturday evening and often continued until 5 o'clock on Sunday morning. It was pointed out that the club premises were surrounded by illicit liquor dens, and it was alleged that drunken Natives were often seen coming out of the club.[10]

But interference could take different forms. Ten years later, for example, even the elite Inchcape Hall was compelled by the Johannesburg City Council to implement earlier closing times, including a Saturday-night shutdown at 11.50 p.m., to preserve the dignity of the colonial sabbath.[11]

For Africans taking part in nocturnal cultural activities, events that lasted the entire night were of course a safe way of avoiding the night curfew. The effect of early closing, therefore, necessitated another bureaucratic infamy: the night pass. A document that could be issued only by authorised persons, its possession was essential to musicians and audience alike if they were to return home without risk of arrest. Often these passes were issued only at the end of the event, creating a logjam for those in the rush to get them, and compounding the indignity of having to carry the document at all. Witness to one of these occasions was a black American political scientist, Ralph Bunche, who visited South Africa in 1937 and frequented the entertainment halls in central Johannesburg. One of his diary entries reads:

> It is pitiful to see the scores of natives, including the entertainers and the bandsmen, crowd around the secretary's counter after the function asking for 'special passes' so they can get home safely. Lithebe writes the passes out for: 'Willie', 'Lucy', 'May', 'George', etc.[12]

---

10 *UWB* 29 September 1923.
11 *BW* 14 January 1933.
12 Robert R. Edgar, *An African American in South Africa: The Travel Notes of*

But even here there was no real security, as sometimes, without warning, the police would swoop early. 'Palm' Mochumi recalled that the police 'used to sometimes come to the halls and stop the dance and ask for night pass: then those who got the night pass are safe, those who got no night pass are all arrested'.[13]

The night pass was of course simply a refinement. What was fundamental was the odious pass system itself, which governed the lives of Africans in the towns, and which affected aspirant professional musicians in particular ways.

In order to reside legally in the towns, Africans had to have 'legitimate' employment – and this often meant musicians had to find some kind of regular (non-musical) daytime job simply in order to qualify for a pass. So their real work, making music, would then begin after hours, after a day's work. To make matters worse, these 'legal' day jobs were typically poorly paid, especially in relation to what a musician could make as a member of a thriving dance band. Trumpeter Edward ('Boetie Vark') Sililo, for instance, recalled that in the 1930s the weekly wage from his daytime job was between seven-shillings-and-sixpence, while during the same period, as a member of the legendary Jazz Maniacs, he made a guinea a night, six nights a week.

After some years, however, Sililo managed to get a 'daily labour permit' – a change in the details in his pass – which now registered his employment simply as 'musician', and thus permitted him to give up his daytime job. But the procedure for obtaining the permit was as bizarre as it was humiliating, for an outcome that was always uncertain. Sililo remembers:

> *Well, you had to prove you were a musician, and if you were a plumber you had to prove you were a plumbing man. They took me to another place and I was told to play a piano. And, well, it's Afrikaner people: you play 'Sarie Marais' and they are very happy. ... 'Kom spiel "Sarie Marais", jong!' [hums] 'Nee man, jy ken! Kom!' ... You just had to go do that, and when you come back, 'Ja, hy's 'n musikant, man!' And then they give it. [laughs] ... And many of us could get these passes, and we used to help the other guys and tell them, 'Oh no, you just tell them you're this, and you play what they [want] you to play.' Be-*

Ralph J. Bunche, Athens and Johannesburg, 1992, p207. Bunche had earned a doctorate from Harvard University in 1934 for his study of French colonial administration. His visit to South Africa was part of a two-year world tour.

13 Cited in Koch, *Doornfontein and its African Working Class, 1914-1935*, p230.

cause they'll ask you to play. 'Jy moet spiel! "Die Hand Vol Vere", jong!' Now if you don't know "Die Hand Vol Vere" – 'Jy's nie 'n musikant nie!' You must play an Afrikaner song. There you are, sign! Got my credentials: from there I was a musician.[14]

If bureaucrats had the power to make 'a musician', or musical career, by dispensing a pass, or to ruin a career by withholding one, their control of the gateway to international opportunity – the passport – gave them another power just as great. In 1937, for instance, one of the country's leading vaudeville troupes was poised to make their first trip to Europe. Led by Esau and later Isaac Mtethwa, they were the remarkable Lucky Stars, a Natal-based group who made famous a kind of vaudeville heavily dependent on 'ethnic' traditions. Overseas horizons began to beckon soon after they met Bertha Slosberg, a spirited and courageous young Russian-born impresario who spent her later childhood and early adulthood in South Africa. Slosberg was one of the first whites – and certainly the first white woman – to become professionally involved with urban black popular music and culture. She firmly believed, in keeping with the liberal political views of the day, that her activities, especially those bringing black culture to white audiences, helped to undermine racial bigotry and assist black advancement.[15]

Slosberg had already had a major success with the Lucky Stars in the Durban City Hall by the time she began preparing to take them, and a young singer known simply as 'Ou Bles', abroad. Preparations included making applications for passports for the group. The planned tour generated some interest among the white community, some members of whom were moved to express their minds on this topic in letters to the press. One letter – 'typical of the many that followed', according to Slosberg – expressed the hope that the government would forbid any adventure of the sort being contemplated, since '[t]aking aborigines to London or other European capitals has not been very productive of any happy results in the past'. More precisely, 'Negro musicians' tended to behave badly in Europe and, most important, 'the class of person they come in contact with is not such as to improve their estimate of white people, which is low enough already.'[16]

---

14 Author's interview: Edward Sililo, Johannesburg 1 December 1986. Both 'Sarie Marais' and 'Die Hand vol Vere' are well-known traditional Afrikaans songs (the melody of the former, however, is adapted from Sep Winner's popular Scottish song, '[Sweet] Ellie Rhee').
15 For details about Bertha Slosberg, see her account of the years she spent in South Africa: *Pagan Tapestry*, London, 1939.
16 Slosberg, *Pagan Tapestry*, pp217-8.

Marabi Nights

Despite her sense that many South Africans shared such views, Slosberg remained optimistic 'that the Government would not evince similar stupidity'. Her, and the group's, hopes were soon dashed: the passports were refused without explanation, and the chance for the Lucky Stars or 'Ou Bles' to go overseas never again returned.[17]

The denial of an enabling document (a passport, a pass, a licence); the fear, or reality, of harassment or arrest: urban black popular musicians experienced these and similar kinds of repression as a formal, or legal, policing of their culture by white authority. But there were other kinds of policing that were less formal – or at least began as such, before the might of the state's legal apparatus was marshalled for assistance. Perhaps the most striking of these developed as a direct result of competition between black musicians and their white counterparts.

The rapid growth of black swing bands in the 1930s, parallel to the demise of *marabi* culture, put such confrontation unmistakably on the agenda, especially as laws forbidding blacks to perform in white venues were not yet in place. Both the Jazz Maniacs and the Merry Blackbirds, for example, had damaging encounters with white musicians in the early 1940s. In one instance, the Maniacs had been booked to play for an extended season at the Log Cabin, a well-known Johannesburg nightclub, as a cabaret band who would play a short set while the main band, who were white, were taking a break.

But the Maniacs' popularity among the white clientele grew, and at the insistence of the audiences they began to play for longer. The white band complained to the club management – and the Maniacs lost the contract. 'We were out now, man', Edward Sililo recalled. 'We were told we can't play for the European because we're taking the European bands' and the European musicians' jobs'.[18] Or as pianist Jacob Moeketsi somewhat more pointedly put it, the white musicians 'were antipathetically disposed ... We, the Jazz Maniacs, used to put them out good – throw them into the shade – and that's not nice, you know'.[19]

Yet as this story begins to suggest, getting rid of a black band often did not suit the clientele, and therefore the financial interests of the management – quite apart from the obvious fact that the black bands were to be hired more cheaply. In such situations, an imaginative compromise could sometimes be found, as Peter Rezant, former leader of the Merry Blackbirds, remembered. Faced with musicians' union complaints that

---

17 Slosberg, *Pagan Tapestry*, p. 243. David Coplan's assertions that Slosberg and the Lucky Stars did go to London, that 'for reasons that are unclear, the tour was a failure', and that 'the troupe disbanded in London', are thus totally without foundation. See Coplan, *In Township Tonight!*, p127.
18 Author's interview: Edward Sililo, Johannesburg, 1 December 1986.
19 Interview by Eddie Koch: Jacob Moeketsi, Johannesburg, 26 June 1980.

the Blackbirds were 'putting white musicians out of jobs', one inventive club manager reassured a white band, whom he had booked for three months, that he would never allow a black band to put them out of a job. Far from it: he would pay the white band their full fee even if they chose to play for only one hour. But he then also hired the Blackbirds to be ready to step in the moment the white band took the early ride home, and to play for the rest of the night.[20]

As time passed, however, the white musicians were to develop more pernicious means of dealing with their black competitors. One of these involved an increasingly cynical use of the musicians' unions. The activities of the racially exclusive Johannesburg Musicians' Union, for example, are a case in point.

During the early 1940s, minutes of the union's meetings are replete with references to what are termed 'Native Bands', and the continuing problem of their being booked to play in white clubs. For union members, the habit of black dance bands 'being allowed to play for Europeans [sic] functions' was a 'growing evil' which had to be 'combatted'; accordingly, it was the subject of a great deal of discussion and correspondence. Ideas for dealing with the menace included a proposal that 'any member of the Union engaging Natives for Dance Bands should be liable to punishment under our rules' (or, in another version, 'should be asked to resign').

Vigilant even about what happened outside its sphere of operation, this union, which later changed its name to the Transvaal Musicians' Union, intervened when it heard that an up-country black band had been booked to play at a nightclub in Durban. The union wrote promptly to the Town Clerk of Durban, who was evidently most happy to co-operate: a subsequent meeting heard that 'the proposed Native Band for Durban had not been engaged, and further the band would not be sent to Durban'.

Such blows to the black bands were real achievements for the white union's members – not least because they usually meant, as a later minute records, that the union 'had been successful in getting the band replaced by a European band'. Predictably, in his Annual Report for the year 1942-43, the union's secretary summed up some of these achievements with a note of satisfaction:

> Recently the Committee had to handle the question of the employment of Native Bands in European places of entertainment. We interviewed the authorities and with their assistance we have succeeded to date, in preventing this form of competition

---

20 Author's interview: Peter Rezant, Riverlea, 3 June 1984.

from continuing. We are sure that members will agree with the action that we have taken.[21]

But the battle against the black bands was not over. The *coup de grâce* was still to come – and it arrived, appropriately, by way of an intervention from the state. As if not satisfied with the headway made so far, the white bands now found themselves bolstered by a another weapon: the liquor laws. Rezant observed wryly:

> *The white musicians: ja, they dictated the terms... The white man has got a voice, you see. So whenever we appeared they would oppose us, until the law was read that blacks shall not play at any place of entertainment where liquor is served.*[22]

In fact, it was not so much a case of a new law being 'read', as of a recent one being invoked. The Liquor Amendment Act of 1934 had prohibited the presence of any 'native, Asiatic or coloured' persons on 'white' liquor-licensed premises unless they were male, over the age of 18, and employed for the purpose of 'cleaning' or 'conveying';[23] but it was some years before this law was rigorously enforced against the black bands. Whether, as Rezant believes, white musicians had a hand in the creation or implementation of the new liquor laws, or whether these were simply devised by a state looking after broader white interests, one thing is certain. For the white bands, the laws played directly into their hands, while for the black bands, as Rezant bluntly puts it, the laws 'simply blotted us out'.[24]

In the short term, the consequences of these various assaults on the black bands included, most obviously, the loss of lucrative contracts. Bad as that was, the long term consequences were even more crippling. First, the number of well-paying venues where they could play legally was severely curtailed. Second, offers of extended bookings from owners of white venues, liquor-licensed or not, virtually dried up, and the bands could now only be used as what Silgee called an occasional 'attrac-

---

21 Official minute books, and files of annual reports and other documents, of the Johannesburg Musicians' Union, in the possession of the South African Musicians' Union (Johannesburg office). The Johannesburg Musicians' Union became the Transvaal Musicians' Union in July 1965, and then, through amalgamation, the South African Musicians' Union in September 1983.
22 Interview by Eddie Koch: Peter Rezant, Johannesburg, 22 June 1980.
23 For fuller details see the Liquor Act 30 of 1928, as amended by Section 24 of the Liquor Amendment Act 41 of 1934. I am grateful to Nick Smythe of the Department of Public Law at the University of Natal, Durban, for assistance in locating the relevant statutes.
24 Interview by Eddie Koch: Peter Rezant, Johannesburg, 22 June 1980.

tion'.[25] Third, restricted increasingly to the odd one-night gigs, the black bands found themselves – especially in comparison with their white counterparts – gradually being forced back into the amateur status which they had fought so hard to overcome. Fourth, with the possibility of a livelihood as professionals now harder to sustain, musicians who had hoped to relinquish their non-musical daytime jobs now found themselves unable to do so; and those who had already done so had to face the real possibility of having to go back to daytime employment. Fifth, the black bands were steadily driven out of the inner city and back into the impoverished townships. And sixth, for bands that had prided themselves on the internationalism of their repertoires and abilities, the damage to their morale was severe. As Rezant says:

Many people didn't believe, but particularly foreigners couldn't believe, that we were what they would call a gig band. A one-night band, you know, a one-night-stand band, and things like that. For a band of our class![26]

So the war waged by the white musicians against the black bands was not only a series of grim and sordid battles; it also produced spoils that totally favoured the aggressors and left the victims beleaguered and undermined. Only once, apparently, did a battle between these competitors, waged in the most bizarre circumstances, result in a different outcome. The occasion, as Sililo remembered it,[27] was precipitated by a dispute over the use of the Jazz Maniacs' name. A white band laying claim to the same name threatened to sue the black band for the right to its exclusive use. Their initial argument, according to Sililo, was that the black group would 'spoil the name', and that in any case they had no historic right to it:

And then we said no, this is our name, and [they] said it's their name. We said, well we've been playing from the 1920s: when did you start your band? It was realised they started very late.

Evidently the white band then based their case on a narrower proposition: that what 'spoiling the name' meant was that the (black) Jazz Maniacs were unable to read staff notation (and were presumably therefore an inferior band). Indignant, the black Maniacs accepted the challenge, and agreed to a procedure for breaking the deadlock.

Though it is not clear whether or not the matter actually came before the court (Sililo claimed that it did, but efforts to trace the case through court records have failed), the agreement was that the dispute would be

---

25 Interview by Tim Couzens: Wilson Silgee, Johannesburg, 22 May 1979.
26 Author's interview: Peter Rezant, Riverlea, 23 June, 1985.
27 Author's interview: Edward Sililo, Johannesburg, 1 December 1986.

settled by having the bands publicly demonstrate their reading skills in a contest on the lawns outside the Johannesburg Supreme Court. Further, it was agreed to have the bands conducted by an experienced, independent conductor, who would also act as expert adjudicator. The person selected for the job was Charles Manning, also known as 'the Svengali of Music', then director of the Colosseum Orchestra in Johannesburg and at that time the city's best-known conductor.[28] As the crowds gathered in the city centre, Manning took the bands through their paces, first the white and then the black. Sililo recounted that as

> *the European band was packing, we were playing on. And you know, the people moving up and down. ... Wow! The traffic was stopped both sides! No cars could go down this way and it was just the people moving there. Traffic cops were this side and that side, stopping the cars from turning left in the street.*[29]

It was clear for all to see, said Sililo, that 'we were reading as well as they did'; and when at the end Charles Manning gave his decision, he found in favour of the black Jazz Maniacs.

Internal repression: Class and Gender

If the first broad category of musical repression suffered by city blacks derived from hostile forces external to their own community, the second, by contrast, was the consequence of incipient class divisions within the urban black community itself. Specifically, it was linked to the emergence of a growing petty-bourgeois class who derived many of their values from white middle-class models, and who believed that these values were essential to its notions of social and political advancement.

This second category of repression differed from the first also in its mode of operation. Instead of hostile legislation, it involved, rather a broad-ranging ideological campaign – to win over the minds and passions of a young and susceptible stratum of city dwellers, and to protect nascent black petty-bourgeois values from being infected by the values of a dynamic, mercurial and irreverent working class.

Undoubtedly, this initiative by sectors of the black petty-bourgeoisie gained enormous bolster from a liberal reform movement among South African whites in the 1920s. Dedicated to attenuating the threat of communist influence among urban blacks, the liberals used a number of ploys – including the promise of housing reform – to seduce the black petty-bourgeoisie away from too close an identification with the working

---

28 For these descriptive details about Charles Manning, I am indebted to the late Ronald Ballantine.
29 Author's interview: Edward Sililo, Johannesburg, 1 December 1986.

class. More to the present point, the liberals, greatly aided by representatives from the American Board of Missions, also helped to inculcate a belief among petty-bourgeois blacks that their political progress rested crucially on the acquisition of Western cultural refinements: indeed, that their very future depended on their achievements in literature, music and art.[30]

In this climate, *marabi* came in for especially vituperative treatment from ministers of the church, teachers, newspaper columnists, some parents, and other self-appointed guardians of the common weal. Branding *marabi* as an 'evil', a 'disturbance' and 'a great menace to the community', their criticism was ostensibly motivated by such issues as the propensity for *marabi* dances to lead to 'scuffles', 'violence', 'lawlessness' and 'intoxication'.[31]

But such concerns masked, and were prompted by, a deeper worry, which did sometimes openly declare itself: the worry that, for at least that class of blacks who felt upward social and political mobility to be within their grasp if they played their hand correctly, the culture of *marabi* would 'create the wrong impressions'.[32] For if, as one letter-writer to *Bantu World* put it in 1937, 'we are making headway' towards 'civilisation', then the danger of *marabi* was that it would 'retard our steady progress' precisely because of its 'backwardness' and 'paganism'.[33] *Marabi* had become popular among working-class youth, the 'refuse and dregs' of society;[34] at the very least, it should not be permitted to contaminate the more 'respectable' classes and jeopardise their ambitions.

Certainly, antidotes to this menace were widely touted: they included, though not always simultaneously, middle-class cultural institutions such as the Pathfinders (Boy Scouts), the *makwaya* tradition of mixed-voice choral singing, and the annual eisteddfod. But always playing a primary role was an ideological campaign seeking to castigate *marabi* as pernicious to progressive black interests. Thus in 1923, for instance, eminent cultural commentator R.R.R. Dhlomo, writing in *Ilanga Lase Natal* under his pen name 'Rollie Reggie', chose to scare his readers by characterising *marabi* as containing an almost cosmological threat:

---

30 See for instance Koch, *Doornfontein and its African Working Class, 1914-1935*, especially pp157-166; and Tim Couzens, '"Moralizing leisure time": the transatlantic connection and black Johannesburg 1918-1936', in Marks and Rathbone, *Industrialisation and Social Change in South Africa*, pp314-337.
31 *BW* 28 May 1932, and 2 November 1940.
32 *UWB* 11 November 1932.
33 *BW* 29 March 1937.
34 *BW* 29 March 1937.

> *Flies and bugs seem to be returning in full power. The atmosphere, too, seem [sic] to be laden with tantalizing density of – I don't know.*
>
> *Once again oTulandivile [marabi] are reviving with remarkable velocity. Down Malay Camp we can hear young Africans playing on the organ as if bent on hammering it to extinction.*
>
> *... in short, the air that once rang with the sweet delight of song, became as solemn as an owl's grave, if you know it...*
>
> *Recently the Rand is experiencing fearful earth-tremors and we naturally resort to prayers that we may be spared from the grim death of being buried alive.*[35]

The threat of destruction was a theme taken up again and again, in different ways. Dhlomo himself, in *An African Tragedy*, a novel published in 1928, tells the pathetic story of a young teacher who goes to Johannesburg to earn money for the bride-price for his intended marriage. But a friend takes him to Prospect Township, where he falls prey to *marabi*.

> *The room in which they found themselves was already half full with people of both sexes. The air was reeking with the evil smell of drinks and perspirations. As they entered, Robert shivered involuntarily. He had not bargained for such a scene of pleasure.*
>
> *At one end of the room an organ was being hammered by a drunken youth. Couples – literally fastened to each other – were swaying giddily wildly, to this barbaric time. In this mood young girls are deflowered in their youth. ...*
>
> *Robert Zulu was now lost. From that night, he had drunk and drunk until he became a hopeless drunkard. His physical health was now impaired. He mixed with loose women. ... The _____ Hall was now his favourite place of amusement.*[36]

Worse is to follow. Robert contracts a venereal disease. The couple's child is born blind, the child dies, the mother collapses into atheistic despair, and Robert is attacked by *tsotsis* (gangsters).

Yet tales of this kind were far from being merely the invention of educated literati. Within the socio-economic class who believed their interests would best be served by distancing themselves as far as possible from *marabi*, and by doing as much as possible to make it difficult for that subculture to survive, tales even more outlandish seem to have circulated freely – and not as fiction, but as historical 'fact'.

---

35 *ILN* 5 October 1923.
36 R.R.R. Dhlomo, *An African Tragedy*, Lovedale, South Africa, n.d., pp6-11.

Music and Repression

One such myth was told to me as recently as 1986 by former vaudeville singer Tommy 'China' Beusen; and it is particularly striking, not only because it is partly autobiographical, but also because it was told with a passionate conviction seemingly undiminished, either by the passing years, or by the fact that he had been living abroad (in England) for decades.

Born in 1914, Beusen was a member, in the 1930s, of the famous Africans' Own Entertainers and the hugely celebrated Darktown Strutters; and his story concerned a girl he once knew, a regular participant at *marabi* parties until, quite suddenly, she died. Because the girl was well known, her funeral was well attended. But the funeral turned out to be not so much a peaceful laying of the dead to rest, as an occasion for supernatural terror. The procession had reached the graveyard when the crowd was suddenly startled by a banging and a ghastly shouting from within the casket:

'Open up! Open up the coffin!' She hit the coffin. 'Open up! Open up! Open up! Open!' Everybody ran like mad. Only the mother was sitting there: 'Oh please open up, my child is alive! Please come back!' These guys had to come back and open the coffin. [The girl] says ... 'Oh my God, marabi! *There are So-, So-and-so and So-and-so are all there, in the fire. I was nearly roasted, and told to come back and tell you. Ah! No more* marabi *for me! You – stop* marabi!' *... She was alive and she was telling them, 'Oh! It's terrible things that I've seen! People burning, and all that! ... I've come to tell you – oh my goodness, this* ndunduma *[*marabi*]! Ndunduma is no good!'*[37]

If the ideological campaign against *marabi* could be conducted – as our examples have illustrated – through, *inter alia*, the expressing of opinions, the telling of stories, or the making of myths, then so too, and perhaps with particular efficacy, could this be done through the singing of songs. It is no surprise, then, to discover that those popular music-makers oriented towards more petty-bourgeois values made, borrowed, sang, rearranged or recorded songs expressive of the appropriate attitudes.

One such song is *'Iqilika'*, the name given to a strong home-brew that was well known within *marabi* subculture. First recorded in 1930 by the great Griffiths Motsieloa (vaudeville entertainer and manager of both the Darktown Strutters and the Pitch Black Follies) with Ignatius Monare, the song was popular enough in the 1930s to be arranged for a jazz band by J.C. Mavimbela's Rhythm Kings. And they included it in their

---
37 Author's interview: Tommy Beusen, London, 28 April 1986.

live broadcast in September 1935 when they were at the height of their fame. It is a poignant catalogue of loss, alluding to the daughters, sons, fathers and mothers who come to the big city and are lost forever to *iqilika* and (by implication) *marabi*:

> Ziphina intombi
> uphina unyana
> ziphina iingwevu
> zezwe le Afrika?
> Ziphina intombi
> baphina oonyana
> iphina iingwevu
> zezwe le Afrika?
> Uphina uma uphina utata?
> Uphi?
> Wavela
> bavele bafele Rawutini.
> Iphina iqilika
> iphina?
> Iphina iqilika?
> Nantsiya iqilika
> nantsiya nantsiya.

> Where are the maidens
> where is the son
> where are the grey old men
> of the country of Africa?
> Where are the maidens
> where are the sons
> where are the grey old men
> of the country of Africa?
> Where is my mother?
> where is my father?
> Where are they?
> They came
> they just died in Johannesburg.
> Where is the *iqilika*
> where is it?
> Where is the *iqilika*?
> There's the *iqilika*
> there it is, there it is[38]

---

38 Motsieloa and Monare: '*Iqilika*' (Singer GE3).

Music and Repression

Another song with a similar intention is *'Sasithunywe Abazali'*, once sung by a mixed-voice group known as The Flying Birds. Here, however, the focus is still sharper: both *marabi* and a slum area of Johannesburg where it flourished are explicitly evoked:

> Sasithunywe abazali
> Ukufuna umntakababa.
> Sasimthanda umntaka
> baba eGoli.
> Sasimthanda umntakababa lona.
> Washiya isikhala esikhulu ekhaya.
> Safikake kwesikhulu isiteshi sase 'Josi.'
> Bathi abanye, 'uma nimfuna, hambani eMaleyikamu.'
> Sayake, safika sathola impi enkulu.
> Sase siyambonake ephakathi kwesixuku.
> Kwaqhamuka onongqayi,
> Yachitheka impi leyo.
> Sase sithi, 'siyamfuna.'
> Sathi, 'uphi? uyephi?'
> Bathi, 'nangu kuMarabi.'
> Safika edushalaza, egxamalaza.
> Kukhala ulugumbukazi, olukhulukazi oludumayo.
> Kusithiwa, 'nguMarabi, nguMarabi.'

> We were sent by our parents
> To search for our father's child.
> In 'Goli'.
> We loved our father's child.
> We loved this father's child,
> He left a big gap at home.
> We then arrived at the huge station in 'Jozi'.
> Some of them said: 'If you want him, go to Malay Camp.'
> We went, and when we arrived we got involved in a mob fight.
> And we caught sight of him amongst the mob.
> The policemen came
> And the mob dispersed.
> Then we said: 'We want him.'
> We said: 'Where is he? Where has he gone?'
> They said: 'Here he is at the *marabi*.'
> We found him jiving and jumping –
> The big resounding organ was playing.
> It was said to us: 'This is *marabi*, this is *marabi*.'[39]

---

39 The original lyrics are quoted from Hugh Tracey, *The Lion on the Path and*

But if *marabi* was first in the firing line, it did not stand there alone. Not too far behind stood – for a while at least – jazz and even ragtime, castigated with articulate rancour on grounds not very dissimilar from those which underpinned the attack on *marabi*. Both bandleader Peter Rezant and Pitch Black Follies singer Lindi Makhanya have testified that in many petty-bourgeois homes in the 1910s and 1920s, ragtime and jazz were roundly detested and discouraged.

This was still happening in Lindi Makhanya's parental home by as late as the mid-1920s, when her aunt would sometimes play ragtime pieces on the 'baby grand'. But her father disapproved, and he and her aunt clashed. 'No, man!' he would say. 'You mustn't play that type of thing ... it's wrong!'[40]

The situation was no different in the home of M.B. Yengwa, who grew up in Natal in the 1920s and 1930s with parents he described as having 'middle-class aspirations'. (Yengwa became a lawyer, as his parents had wished, and later rose to prominence within the African National Congress.) As typically happened in the homes of Yengwa's social class, his parents were deeply suspicious of jazz and discouraged their children from learning a jazz instrument: they feared 'you'd in fact become *isibhunguka* – the one who has deserted his home through wrong associations.'[41] By contrast of course Western-style classical music, or choir singing, as he remembered, bore no such stigma. And yet discouragement could never be enough. Jazz had not yet found favour among those sectors of the white ruling group whose political patronage was being sought; so if the fears of the black petty bourgeoisie were to be allayed and their interests pursued, jazz and the subculture that fostered it would still need to be more securely incriminated.

The ideologists soon lighted upon a new and fertile line of attack: jazz could be *pathologised*. Branded a disease with pollutants so noxious that contamination by them would have the most dire consequences, jazz could readily be characterised as out of bounds, except under the strictest controls. R.R.R. Dhlomo's article, 'The Jazzing Craze', written for *Ilanga* in August 1927, is typical of this approach. Jazz was a 'sickness' and a 'disease'; but one so 'infectious' and so easily 'contracted' that it had led to a 'plague'. The symptoms were a 'craze', a 'madness' and 'a fantastic longing', which held its 'victims' in an 'octopus-like grasp'.[42]

Other African Stories, London, 1967. 'Goli' (the place of gold) and 'Jozi' are colloquial names for Johannesburg. The slum area referred to is of course Malay Camp.

40 Author's interview: Lindi Makhanya, Soweto, 13 February 1987. Interview by Tim Couzens: Peter Rezant, Johannesburg, 29 July 1979.
41 Author's interview: M.B. Yengwa, London, 8 April 1986.
42 *ILN* 5 August 1927.

Nearly five years later, leading elite music critic Mark Radebe was still identifying the same pathology. Writing in *Umteteli wa Bantu*, he implied that the music's virus-like qualities revealed themselves in its 'intoxicating, nerve-flaying influence', and its tendency to act 'as a million whips upon human emotions'; its 'terrible and destructive' consequences were to be seen in the symptoms of nothing less than 'tremens agitans and outright epilepsy'.[43] Yet on occasion, the need for disease as a metaphor for jazz fell away, as real disease itself took over. A columnist in *Ilanga*, for instance, described a sick, broken victim of – as he believed – the jazz halls or other nefarious haunts:

> *In the Mayville slum along the main road to Maritzburg, I used to see a Native degenerate – a lost sheep. He was, I believe, the result of the night dances, three-card trick or a product of the motor-bus 'crooks' such as one may see on any week-end evening in Grey Street or around the Dance Halls. He used to sit there along the road like the 'Lazarus' of old with sores on his hands and legs, impotent and begging.*[44]

Whether or not the pathologisers of jazz in South Africa knew that this was precisely the way jazz was portrayed in the United States after the First World War, is not clear. But it is remarkable that the same medical and psychological discourse was used against jazz in these two societies. In 1922, for instance, the *New York American* ran an article alleging that moral disaster was on its way because of the 'pathological, nerve-irritating, sex-exciting music of jazz orchestras'. The report cited a study by the Illinois Vigilance Association, which in Chicago alone had 'traced the fall of 1 000 girls in the last two years to jazz music', which it described as 'insidious' and 'neurotic'.[45]

Appeals to pathology were of course merely an embellishment. Behind them lay a very real fear of the harm that jazz would do to the norms and institutions of a social group looking out for its future in specific ways. In South Africa such fears were often articulated by way of cultural comparisons. Western classical music, in R.R.R. Dhlomo's view, always had 'soothing and inspiring effects', which could 'tone' and 'modulate' the 'natural impulse of the young'; jazz, by contrast, was inseparable from 'suggestive movements and passionate expressions'. What then, he wondered, 'can we expect from a boy or girl who only dreams and visualises such worded songs as 'Fondle me closer, dear heart'?[46]

---

43 *UWB* 18 June 1932.
44 *ILN* 9 September 1932.
45 *New York American* 22 June 1922. Cited in Tirro, *Jazz: A History*, p156.
46 *ILN* 5 August 1927.

Marabi Nights

Western 'civilization' and 'progress' themselves served as other points of comparison – though the ironies involved here were seldom lost on even the most sycophantic of commentators. Jazz and jazz dancing had roots in the West but, as one *Ilanga* columnist noted, among Africans 'scores of promising young people ... have been dragged down into the mire of evildom by this dancing.' There was a hard lesson to learn:

> *We are after progress and not degeneration. One of our best Native brains has said, 'Let us copy from the whiteman only that which is good', but it appears we are also entangling ourselves with his vices. Better forms of recreation could be devised, which would be of a constructive nature.*[47]

Or, as a letter-writer to *Bantu World* vehemently put it:

> *Married men are not ashamed to leave their wives at home and attend these dances where they dance with unmarried ladies, and unmarried ladies do not unfortunately have the pluck to enquire from these gentlemen about their wives. Is this civilisation? If it is let us get fuller information.*[48]

That question – 'Is this civilisation?' – was not a rhetorical device. For a significant sector of black urbanites after all, civilisation, in Western terms, was a founding assumption that not only grounded many others, but also laid the basis for the hopes and aspirations of a way of life. But civilisation, in this discourse, did duty in another way too: it foregrounded the position of women as the wives and mothers of the nation, the selfless nurturers and noble protectors of home and realm, and the guardians of civilised society. As Kathy Eales has argued, these particular attitudes to women derived, in part, from ruling-class Edwardian thought, which was introduced into South Africa by the English missionaries.

Clearly harmonious with the 'civilising' appeals being made to urban blacks by the liberal reform movement, these attitudes resurfaced among the African petty-bourgeoisie in, for example, the pervasive belief that 'no nation can rise higher than its womanhood', or in an injunction such as the one issued by D.D.T. Jabavu in a speech in 1920: 'If we mean to rise in this world and to command the respect of other nations we must begin by raising up our women'.[49]

In a climate of deep petty-bourgeois mistrust of jazz, such attitudes inevitably had the effect of targetting single women, above all other

---

47 *ILN* 12 November 1926.
48 *BW* 30 December 1933. (Emphasis added.)
49 Kathy Eales, 'Patriarchs, Passes and Privilege', in Bonner, Hofmeyr, James and Lodge, *Holding their Ground*, p117.

groups in society, to bear the brunt of ongoing and hostile admonitions about jazz. Moreover, the discourse positioned women – and especially single women – in two quite contradictory locations: at one moment as helpless victims of jazz and ragtime, and at the next as responsible actors who should have known better.

Concerns about women's 'virtue' were central. In a letter to the women's section of *Bantu World*, for instance, one correspondent confessed to his long-standing fear of jazz dances and wondered whether 'a girl who leaves home in the night [to attend a dance] can come back home in the morning feeling the same purity of heart as she had when she left'. Another correspondent thought that the root of the problem was to be found in the question 'whether you can look for a marriage partner in a place where proper introductions are seldom observed'. Critic Walter Nhlapo, developing this theme in the same newspaper, noted that since 'girls come without partners and expect to pick them up there ... they are open victims to all evils'. In similar vein, R.R.R. Dhlomo warned his *Ilanga* readers that not even the 'air in the hall [is] ... conducive to pure thoughts and desires', and meditated upon the wisdom of the 'Fox-trot song which says: "If you wish to keep your wife at home never teach her how to dance"'.[50]

While many different kinds of danger seemed to follow women to the dance halls, one of the more common was thought to be the danger of being 'cheapened'. Women who, by dancing with various men, became 'everybody's partner', instantly also became 'as cheap as monkey nuts which are sold at a penny a paperbag' – with the consequence (in a different metaphor) that '[s]hop-soiled girls, like shop-soiled goods, are offered at a much cheaper price than marriage'.[51]

Fortunately, in a world so full of jazz, ragtime and other threats to a woman's character and good name, advice about the right behaviour was always close to hand. A 'doctor', for instance, writing a women's-page column in *Umteteli* in December 1936, addressed his advice to 'all the young, developing women who will shortly take their place as the proud mothers of the sons of our nation'. His recommendations left no space at all for smoky halls, jazz and all-night dances:

> *Cultivate a clean body and clean mind. Be in the fresh air all you can, sleep with the window wide open, clean your teeth twice a day, have the decayed ones stopped, keep your skin pure and sweet by frequent washing, see that your habits are regular, go to bed in good time, and eat your food slowly. Fill your minds with useful knowledge; learn housekeeping, domestic*

---

50 *BW* 18 January 1936, 13 May 1939, 8 June 1940; *ILN* 19 March 1936.
51 *BW* 4 April 1935, 8 July 1939, 14 December 1940.

economy, cooking and sewing and dressmaking. Make nice friends and beware of companionship with the thriftless and careless.[52]

Changing attitudes

Gradually, with the passage of time, the black elite's negative attitudes towards jazz began to change. The reason for this change is not entirely clear, but can be inferred with some confidence. In the United States, jazz musicians were rising in status within black American culture – so much so that by the late 1920s they were already prestigious and influential figures. For many decades, as we have seen, there had been a history of contact between black South Africans and the United States, and a tendency for black South Africans to make powerful role models of their American counterparts. It was, therefore, inevitable that when black attitudes towards jazz shifted in the United States these changes would eventually have an impact on the African subcontinent. Similarly, softening attitudes to ragtime in South Africa were probably, at least in part, the result of its acceptance among black Americans: without this shift in attitude, it is unlikely that the ragtime songs of Reuben Caluza would have been so admired at home, and still less that they would have been regarded 'as an expression of racial pride' and identified with 'the emerging black nationalist movement in South Africa'.[53]

Aware of course that elite black South African attitudes to jazz were changing as the mid-1930s approached, local commentators said, by way of explanation, that it was the *music* that had changed. Indeed it had – following the United States suit, this was now the 'swing' era – but it is most unlikely that stylistic modifications on their own could have engendered the new critical outlook. Older styles and older perceptions were giving place to newer, and musicians, audiences and commentators alike needed to begin to explain these shifts to themselves and to each other.

In this work of collective rationalisation, one dominant theme, entirely predictably, was that jazz had become more acceptable because it had become more *refined*. 'Refinement' is a highly selective way of understanding the development of American jazz from its New Orleans phase through to the 'swing' era. But it was appropriate, because it clearly sat so well with the overarching project of cultural 'refinement' with which the black petty-bourgeoisie was so preoccupied. And it is no surprise, too, that in this context the sweeter, blander, more Eurocentric society swing bands of the Paul Whiteman variety were often held up for special praise.

---

52 *UWB* 26 December 1936.
53 Erlmann, *African Stars*, p126.

A clear instance of these shifting perceptions and their accompanying rationalisations, is 'Jazzmania', an article by Mark Radebe (writing pseudonomously as 'Musicus'), in *Umteteli* in February 1933. Noting the global spread of the 'crime of jazz', Radebe reassured his readers that '[t]he old jazz of the screeching jazzmaniac will not torture its victims much longer'. The reason for this was the appearance of 'a few minds which had been trained in the better things of music'. Whiteman and Gershwin had 'modified and beautified the jazz orchestra until the results were often surprisingly interesting'. So with jazz 'purifying itself', he and his readers could 'look forward to a time when our eardrums will not be shattered by a pandemonium of horrible noises'. The demise of one of 'the great frauds of the centuries', a music 'for the most part built upon an entirely artificial basis', was clearly a time for celebration: 'King Jazz is dying! His syncopating, brothel-born, war-fattened, noise-drunk [body], is now in a stage of hectic decline'.[54]

Two years later in the same paper, and in similar vein, a columnist writing about the huge popularity of local dance bands, gave a brief history of the jazz band in the United States. For a long time these were the 'noisiest' bands, and were 'often lacking in real musical value'. Even the Original Dixieland Jazz Band was

> uncouth, for at least one of the players did not know a note of music, and the sounds he made often had little to do with the melody in progress. Noise of course was essential in those days and motor horns and revolvers were part of the drummer's outfit.

But now things were different. Paul Whiteman had finally 'showed what could be done with big bands'. The message in all this for South African bands hardly needed spelling out:

> In their attempt to play dance music, they have not yet succeeded in shaking off the conventions of 1912-1920 which demanded that they should make as much noise as possible and be for ever inventing new ear-piercing sounds.[55]

No doubt it was a perception which at least some of the local bands shared. One of these was the elite Merry Blackbirds. After the sort of performance for which the Blackbirds became famous, a *Bantu World* reviewer saluted the group for having proved that, at any dance, 'the discipline of the house' rests on one crucial component – the kind of music the band plays. Some pieces, he asserted, should be avoided: though these are the usually the favourites, they unfortunately 'rouse the

---

54 *UWB* 11 February 1933.
55 *UWB* 10 August 1935.

passions of the audience', and therefore 'wherever and whenever they are played they lead to disorder'.[56]

But bands like the Merry Blackbirds, the reviewer might have gone on to say, were helping to make jazz respectable. And for evidence that they succeeded, one need look no further than a block advertisement placed in the black press in November 1941 by – of all things – the Tea Market Expansion Bureau. Boldly headed 'Now He's The Best Man In The Band', the advertisement foregrounds a large drawing of a black trumpet player, and in cartoon-strip form shows how tea-drinking has not only made him a better member of what is clearly a 'swing' band, but has also given him the power to play crowd-winning solos.[57]

Ludicrous the advertisement may be, but there is no doubt that a dance band musician could only have been used to promote the civilized past-time of tea-drinking if, by the 1940s, 'swing' was fully respectable, and its musicians had become prestigious members of elite black society.

In an environment hostile to it in a number of ways, then, jazz steadily made some gains, though these were clearly of an ideological kind only, and internal to the black community itself: the struggle with external white authority, for autonomy over performance space and time, had resulted in setbacks which were not to be redressed for half a century. Yet after the early 1940s the gains, such as they were, would deepen in significance, as jazz, touched by a new spirit of black militancy, came to assume a role in the struggle for emancipation. Ahead lay a period of 15 or 20 years of vital creativity, a golden era, as it would come to be termed, but also a period of respite before the dark night of the mature apartheid state closed in to smother even that.

---

56 *BW* 9 November 1940.
57 See for instance *BW* 15 November 1941.

APPENDIX
The Cassette:
Marabi Nights[1]

Vaudeville

TRACK 1[2]
Stimela No.1 [The First Train]
Griffiths Motsieloa and Company
Recorded in London, 1931; issued on Singer GE 56

One of the giants of black South African entertainment in the first half of the century, Griffiths Motsieloa was not only a brilliant, prolific and multi-talented performing artist, but also a dynamic and trend-setting entrepreneur. In one of the most famous early exploits of the South African recording industry, Brunswick Gramophone House dispatched him to London in 1930 and again in 1931, where he organized and took part in a number of recordings with other South Africans for the home market – recordings that at once reflected the best of South African vaudeville, made innovations, and set new standards. (Several of these recordings are featured on this cassette.)

---

1 The recorded sources for this cassette were of course 78 r.p.m. shellac records. All these were several decades old, and many were in poor condition. However, wherever possible the disks themselves – and where impossible, taped copies – have been subjected to elaborate mechanical and electronic remastering techniques. Rob Allingham played a vital role in this process.
2 For this and all subsequent tracks, the composer and arranger are unknown unless otherwise indicated.

This particular song makes reference to a long journey, and the 'Emily' to whom it is addressed is Motsieloa's wife: but the symbolism here would not have been lost on Africans working in the towns, most of whom – even if they were not migrants – retained close connections with rural areas. Significantly, the song is polylingual, drawing together several of the languages spoken in a major urban centre such as Johannesburg. The traces of ragtime are deeply characteristic of urban black popular music of the early decades of the century; but a more indigenous call-and-response technique is also evident in this song. The piece briefly surfaced again in 1960, in a version recorded by the Skylarks (a female vocal group led by the young Miriam Makeba), with the title 'Emily' (issued on New Sound GB 3181).

TRACK 2
Sponono naMarabi [Sponono with *Marabi*]
Griffiths Motsieloa and Company
Recorded in London, 1931; issued on Singer GE 67

For a variety of reasons (discussed in the main body of this book), elite performers disdained *marabi* music and its subculture, but were not able to detach themselves wholly from it. This recording is a most remarkable case in point: for here Motsieloa strings together what were arguably the two most famous songs of the entire *marabi* era – and gives to both an aura of refinement that would clearly not have inhered in the originals. The first of them, '*Sponono ndiyeke*' (Sponono leave me alone), is a song of parting, alluding to the hated poll tax whose purpose was to drive men off the land to work on the white-owned farms and mines. ('*Sponono*' is a popular, and normally gender-specific, term of endearment, that a man might use for his girlfriend or wife: 'sweetheart' is an approximate English equivalent.)

Legend has it that the second song (of the two used here) arose in mocking tribute to the man who was the most legendary keyboard player of the *marabi* era. Known as Ntebejana, he was revered for his brilliance as an improviser as much as he was ridiculed for the outrageousness of his alleged physical ugliness. As the song puts it, '*uNtebejana ufana nemfene*' (Ntebejana looks like a baboon) – words that, in Motsieloa's version, release a peal of stylized laughter.

TRACK 3
Tsaba Tsaba ke No.1[3] [*Tsaba Tsaba* is No.1]
Motsieloa's Pitch Black Follies
Recorded in Johannesburg, 1939; issued on Singer GE 853

The most prestigious of the vaudeville troupes, the Pitch Black Follies were formed by Motsieloa in 1936 from the Darktown Strutters – themselves pre-eminent throughout Southern Africa – which he had also managed. Typically, vaudeville troupes had varied repertoires, which made place for neo-traditional songs such as this one. Here the lyrics extol the *tsaba-tsaba*, a popular dance which succeeded the *marabi* dance but used music which employed the same chord structure. The shouted interjections exclaim the name of a famous Johannesburg *marabi* pianist, popularly known as Highbricks.

TRACK 4
Qua qa
William and Wilfred Mseleku
Recorded in Johannesburg, 2 November 1932; issued on HMV GU 107

William Mseleku was one of the country's most admired vaudeville personalities, and leader of the extensively recorded Durban-based troupe, the Amanzimtoti Players (known at various times as the Amanzimtoti Zulu Choir, Mseleku's Party, or the Amanzimtoti Royal Entertainers). He was also the artistic head of one of South Africa's most talented musical families; indeed, family-members made up the core of the troupe. (Today, his pianist and saxophonist-son Bheki, currently based in England, is one of the brightest South African stars in the international jazz firmament.) '*Qua qa*', featuring William and one of his brothers, is a novelty song: the words mean nothing, and their point is simply to present a play on a variety of African 'clicks'. The song achieved considerable popularity: as recently as the 1950s, for instance, some African children in Natal schools were being taught to sing it (though sometimes mistakenly as an example of a 'Bushman' song!).

---

[3] The label incorrectly gives *Tsaba Tsabake No.1*.

TRACK 5
Ndunduma [Minedumps]
Bantu Glee Singers
Recorded in Johannesburg, 16 November 1932; issued on HMV GU 94

Within two years of their founding, the Bantu Glee Singers had made this and more than 40 other records, and had laid the basis for what was to become a long-lived series of tours throughout the country. The troupe's founder was Nimrod Makhanya, whose most important models were the great Natal-based composer, choirmaster and educationist, Reuben Caluza, and his celebrated Double Quartette. Their influence is clearly evident in a recording such as this.

With roots in the cyclical chord-structure of *marabi*, this lively song is named after a *marabi* style developed by Zulu-speaking migrant workers on the gold-mining reef. But its lyrics take a typically middle-class view of *marabi* culture: Johannesburg, with its *ndunduma* (literally, minedumps), overwhelms and corrupts, so that, for example, women take secret lovers.

TRACK 6
Emakhaya[4] [At home]
Snowy Radebe and Company
Recorded in Johannesburg, c.1945; Singer, unissued

Famed for the clarity and warmth of her high soprano, Snowy Radebe was one of the leading singers of the Pitch Black Follies; and her 'Company' – which existed only within the confines of the recording studio – consisted simply of members of the Follies recording under the name of one of their most valued stars. Jazz musician and journalist Todd Matshikiza once reminisced that though he had heard 'great singers', until he encountered Snowy, he 'had never heard a voice of such great power, range, beauty and sheer magnificence'.[5]

Emakhaya is a concertized version of a song in the style of so-called 'wedding songs' – a popular, neo-traditional genre which comprised both well-known and newly-composed pieces. The spoken dialogue has a young woman, with her luggage, explaining that because of Johannesburg's *tsotsis* (gangsters) she is leaving the city for good; the song itself suggests her happiness at the idea of sleeping *emakhaya* (at home).

---
4 The label incorrectly gives *Makaya*.
5 'Jazz comes to Joburg!', *Drum* July 1957.

TRACK 7
Khanya [Light]
Griffiths Motsieloa and Company
Recorded in London, 1931; issued on Singer GE 32

A large proportion of songs in the vaudeville repertoire owed much less to indigenous than to imported musical styles. That tendency is exemplified in this, and the next two songs in this vaudeville selection, which are therefore 'purer' instances of Western popular styles than most of the syncretic blends exhibited earlier on the tape. Their lyrics, however, still have a very local resonance.

Khanya, for example, is a song whose lyrics reveal underpinnings both in Christian beliefs and in traditional African societies. The 'light' of the title is the light of the bible (as well of the sun, the stars, gold and silver) – but it is also the light that helps one to find a wife and obtain the bride-price necessary in traditional African societies to secure her.

TRACK 8
eGoli[6] [In Johannesburg]
John Mavimbela and Company
Recorded in London, 1931; issued on Singer GE 65

John Mavimbela was best known as a saxophonist and the leader of the famous Rhythm Kings jazz band, which he founded soon after he broke away from the Merry Blackbirds some time between 1933 and 1935.[7]

But he had begun his career as a vaudeville artist, and was in the party co-ordinated by Griffiths Motsieloa for the London recordings in 1931. This song, which emerged from those sessions, relates a tale that would have been familiar enough: while trying to find work, a newcomer to Johannesburg illegally sells a bottle of liquor, is arrested, and suffers the painful experience of being sent to prison.

TRACK 9
Aubuti Nkikho [Brother Nkikho]
Griffiths Motsieloa and Ignatius Monare
Recorded in London, 1930; issued on Singer GE 1

The obsession of black South Africans with American popular music in general, had many consequences for local musical practice. Of these, this song – an imitation of American country music, complete with yodel and Hawaiian guitar – is one of the more curious. But it does not stand alone: black imitations of white country music were fashionable in the early

---

6   The label incorrectly gives *E Goli*.
7   Neither surviving documentation nor oral testimony allows us to specify this date more precisely.

1930s. (And as if to compound the irony, the guitarists are probably two Afrikaans musicians who were in London at the same time as Motsieloa, recording Afrikaans songs for the same company.)

The song is a kind of lament, in which here the essential components are poverty, unemployment, and the wrenching conflict between town and rural life.

TRACK 10
eBhayi[8] [In Port Elizabeth]
Snowy Radebe and Company
Recorded in Johannesburg, c.1945; Singer, unissued

The series of recordings that members of the Pitch Black Follies made under the title of Snowy Radebe and Company reveal, as almost nothing else does, the idiomatic and technical excellence of which the Follies – and other superior troupes – were capable, even when it came to closely imitating foreign styles. *eBhayi* is a fine example: musically, the piece owes nothing to indigenous traditions, and yet its African exponents, singing in Xhosa, deliver a performance that is beautifully crafted in Western terms.

The song celebrates the city of *Bhayi* (more officially known by its colonial name, Port Elizabeth), and exploits the pun suggested by its vernacular name: the similar-sounding *ibhayi* means 'blanket'. Thus *Bhayi*, the city, is declared to be a haven, a place that in comparison to other cities offers solace, strength and warmth – in short, the comfort of a metaphorical *ibhayi*.

---

8 The record label gives an alternative, but less acceptable, notation: *E-Bhai*.

Jazz

TRACK 11
Sbhinono[9] [*Sponono*]
Amanzimtoti Players
Recorded in Johannesburg, 4 November 1932; issued on HMV GU 130 and JP 165

Marabi is the most important single ingredient in the development of a South African jazz style. Though the original *marabi* idiom had a number of distinctive features, it is essentially the harmonic structure that survived, and gave to the subsequent development of South African jazz one of its most characteristic flavours. As such, the relationship between *marabi* and South African jazz is similar to that between the blues and American jazz. Moreover, like the blues, *marabi* uses a cyclical harmonic structure that, in Western terms, would be described as normally consisting of tonic, subdominant and dominant harmonies, frequently represented as seventh-chords. (In the case of *marabi*, this repeating structure consists basically of the following chord sequence, or variants of it: I–IV–I$^6_4$–V.)

But we should not take the blues analogy too far: for example, in the blues the fundamental chords are strung together in a rather different way, leading to a longer internal structure with different emphases; and *marabi* makes no use of 'blue-note' pitch-inflections. As a result, the two styles sound entirely distinct, despite their common origins in the cyclical patterns typical of indigenous African musics.

As the quintessential music of the slumyards, *marabi* in its classic original form was – tragically – never recorded. What were recorded, however, were a number of performances which refracted the early music of the slumyards: in particular, these include *marabi* in imitations,

---

9 The singer uses an unusual pronunciation for *Sponono*: he pronounces it '*Sbhinono*'. The record label, however, incorrectly renders this as *Sibhinono*.

recreations and arrangements – all of them typically performed by elite groups – as well as, though rarely, later survivals of the style. As such, many of these are recordings of great historical importance (a few have already been heard as part of the vaudeville selection on this cassette).

The recording of *Sbhinono*, by the Amanzimtoti Players, which here opens the jazz portion of the cassette, is a good example. Though this is a performance by what was of course a vaudeville group (see the notes for Track 4), it is almost vertainly the earliest recorded simulation of *marabi* piano. The first of the famous *marabi* songs featured in Motsieloa's *Sponono naMarabi* (Track 2) appears here again. Sung at the outset, it gives the piece its title and, more important, 'announces' the piece as a clear evocation of *marabi*. In the slumyards, a hand-held rattle in the form of a tin filled with pebbles provided a percussive effect; here this is rendered by more elaborate means. Even so, the recording is probably only a pale imitation of early *marabi* performance style.

TRACK 12
Evelina
Nkandla[10] Guitar Players
Recorded in Johannesburg, c.1948; issued on Gallotone-Singer GE 975

Marabi is normally associated with the keyboard (piano or pedal organ), but it was also played in the slumyards on guitars. And though its heyday was over by the mid-1930s, forms of it did survive in pockets – in some small towns and semi-rural areas, for example – where social conditions were subject to less rapid change. This recording, by a group named after the Nkandla district of rural Natal, is interesting as one such survival, and as an example of guitar-based *marabi*. Well-known in its day, this particular song is named after the *shebeen* queen who, as the lyrics tell us, was famous for selling brews of remarkable potency.

TRACK 13
Sponono[11]
Jazz Revellers Band
Recorded Johannesburg, 1933; issued on Columbia AE 45

Tracks 2 and 11 were both loosely based on *Sponono ndiyeke*, one of most popular songs of the *marabi* era. Here is yet another such piece, though in this instance the song is worked into a compounded song form typically found in ragtime pieces. Established in 1929 and led by saxophonist Sonny Groenewald, the Jazz Revellers were a coloured band who

---
10 The label uses an older spelling: Nkandhla.
11 The label incorrectly gives *Seponono*.

rank among the earliest black bands to have achieved widespread fame. They were especially in demand to supply music for ballroom dancing.

TRACK 14
Ntebejana[12]
W.P. Zikali
Recorded in Johannesburg, 1933; issued on Columbia AE 45

As already indicated (see the notes for Track 2), *Ntebejana ufana nemfene* was one of the best-known songs of the *marabi* era; and it was named after that subculture's most famous keyboardist. Like many popular *marabi* songs – *Sponono ndiyeke* is by now a familiar example – it was sung, played, arranged, and sometimes even recorded, in numerous versions. The present version is an arrangement for dance band, with the lyrics sung by W.P. Zikali, a well-known elite entertainer, pianist, singer and composer, and a diplomate of Trinity College, London (he held an A.T.C.L.). Though its name is not given on the record label, the band is almost certainly the Jazz Revellers, who are also featured on the previous track.

TRACK 15
iChain Covers[13] [The Chain Covers]
Arranged by Emily Motsieloa (Gallo Music Publishers)
The Merry Blackbirds
Recorded in Johannesburg, c.1934; issued on Singer GE 94

In 1930, Peter Rezant took up a suggestion put to him by Griffiths Motsieloa that, because there were 'no bands' in Johannesburg (by which he meant that the only bands were 'crude' ones), he should start a band of his own.[14]

So Rezant convened a five-piece ensemble which, remarkably for the time, included a woman: the fine pianist Emily Motsieloa, whose husband was Griffiths. They called themselves the Motsieloa Band. By 1932, however, the band, which was expanding in size and reputation, changed its name to the Merry Blackbirds. This title remained for the rest of its decades-long career, and that became the hallmark of one of the most prestigious bands (and certainly the most elite) in the country.

Here the band plays an orchestrated version of a *marabi* tune, whose title, invented by the band, refers to the metal chain-covers that were sometimes added to bicycles to protect the rider's clothes from becoming

---

12 The label gives a less phonetic, and therefore less acceptable, spelling: *Ntebetshana*.
13 The label incorrectly gives *E Chain Covers*.
14 Author's interview: Peter Rezant, Johannesburg, 3 June 1984.

soiled by the chain. Around the time this piece was recorded, these covers were becoming fashionable among 'well-dressed' blacks.[15] Thus, in choosing this title, the Merry Blackbirds added an elite touch to what was at heart a ghetto tune.

Since record companies were notoriously irresponsible about crediting local black composers and arrangers (in similar fashion, royalty payments for black artists simply did not exist), it is today – decades after the event – usually impossible to reconstruct these details. In the case of this recording (and a few others on this cassette), however, I have made an attribution, usually on the basis of information supplied by someone who at the time was involved in, or at least closely concerned with, the recording. Peter Rezant is sure that the arrangement of *iChain Covers* was done by Emily Motsieloa.[16]

TRACK 16
uMajaji[17]
Arranged by Emily Motsieloa (Gallo Music Publishers)
The Merry Blackbirds
Recorded in Johannesburg, 1937; Singer, unissued

Another piece with roots in *marabi* (again in an arrangement by Emily Motsieloa[18]), this was, in its day, one of the most popular numbers in the Merry Blackbirds' repertoire.[19]

Also present here, however, are traces of ragtime rhythms, and the piece is woven from intricate counterpoints in a manner suggestive of Dixieland style. The sung portion is cryptic, unless one knows that in the slumyards illegally-brewed liquor was stored in barrels, which were buried in the ground to avoid police detection. This ploy did not always work – and nor did it always keep the brew safe from thieves, who of course could hardly then be reported to the police. One such thief, in the words of the song, was a certain Majaji, who was now being sought – presumably by the brewers – for his theft.

---

15 Peter Rezant: personal communication, 9 February 1993.
16 Peter Rezant: personal communication, 9 February 1993. Rob Allingham's assistance in this connection is acknowledged.
17 The label gives an alternative, but less acceptable, notation: *U-Majaji*.
18 Peter Rezant: personal communication, 9 February 1993.
19 Author's interview: Peter Rezant, Riverlea, 23 June 1985.

TRACK 17
Woza we Mzala [Come on, everybody]
Composed by Griffiths and Emily Motsieloa (Gallo Music Publishers)
The Merry Blackbirds
Recorded in Johannesburg, 1937; issued on Singer GE 185

During the 1930s, Latin rhythms such as the rhumba entered the mainstream of American popular music through the work of Xavier Cugat and other bandleaders, and soon made an impact on South African music. This piece is an example – and it is one of several recorded by the Merry Blackbirds which show an interest in Latin rhythms. The Dixieland counterpoints are, however, still in evidence; and the exclamations in the recording are shouts of encouragement to others to join in the dance.

Though he undoubtedly composed a great deal more, this is one of the few pieces that we can attribute with any confidence to Griffiths Motsieloa – here in partnership with Emily.[20]

TRACK 18
Marabi No. 2 Jive
Hot Lips Dance Band
Recorded in Johannesburg, c.1945; issued on Rayma RB 5

As the title suggests, this is a piece explicitly in *marabi* style. But it is an *evocation* of the style, rather than simply the thing itself: given both the relatively late date of the recording and the relative complexity of the piano style, this is more likely to be a conscious recreation of the *marabi* idiom than an 'innocent' (and, for its time, unusual) survival of it. In the spoken portion of the recording, the leader refers to the prowess of the group, and introduces them by means of what are probably nicknames. Of the band itself, however, little is known; but the piano style strongly suggests that the pianist is none other than the extraordinary Thomas Mabiletsa, featured later on this cassette as a soloist (Tracks 22 and 23).

---

20 Peter Rezant: personal communication, 9 February 1993.

> **TRACK 19**
> *Mabuza*[21]
> Composed by Willie Gumede[22] (Gallo Music Publishers)
> **Willie Gumede's Swing Band**
> Recorded in Johannesburg, 1945; Singer, unissued
>
> **TRACK 20**
> *Mkhize*[23]
> Composed by Willie Gumede[24] (Gallo Music Publishers)
> **Willie Gumede's Swing Band**
> Recorded in Johannesburg, 1945; issued on Gallotone-Singer GE 942

Though he played several instruments, sang, and led a wide range of bands which made a large number of recordings over many years, neither Willie Gumede nor any of his bands ever achieved the kind of recognition which was their due, and he remains one of the figures in the annals of South African jazz and dance music about whom little is known and virtually no trace exists. (He appears to have originated in Natal's Nkandla district, moved to Johannesburg where he lived in Alexandra Township, and worked for many years as a factory supervisor for Troubadour Records.)[25]

One of the specialities of the group that Gumede called his swing band, exemplified in these two recordings, is a combination of a Dixieland style with the strummed banjo patterns characteristic of the coloured-Afrikaans and white-Afrikaans dance styles known as *tikkiedraai* and *vastrap*. Another distinctive feature is that the band is a small outfit, cultivating a lean and intimate style in many respects quite unlike the bigger, brasher, fuller sound generally sought by the black swing bands of the 1940s. *Mabuza* and *Mkhize* – the titles of the pieces – are well-known Nguni names.

---

21 The label incorrectly gives *Mambuza*.
22 My attribution.
23 The label incorrectly gives *Mkize*.
24 My attribution.
25 I owe this information, obtained with help from Rob Allingham, to Mary Thobei, a retired singer and recording artist who encountered Gumede when she was working for Troubadour in the 1950s and early 1960s.

TRACK 21
Heat Wave
Composed by Irving Berlin (Chappel-Chappel S.A.)
The Merry Blackbirds
Recorded in Johannesburg, 1939; issued on Singer GE 862

'A real hit on the stage', irrespective of whether they played the piece for audiences of blacks or whites: that is how bandleader Peter Rezant remembers the Merry Blackbirds' performances of this piece.[26]

That it should have been so is not surprising. Here was an adaptation of an Irving Berlin classic, featuring fashionable Latin rhythms, and showcasing the crisp, articulate playing of a top local band at the height of its powers – as the recording testifies. The lyrics deliver the band's praises, and are sung by the band-members themselves. The gist of what they say is that in towns throughout the country, people are talking about the Blackbirds!

TRACK 22
Zulu Piano Medley, No.1: Part 1
Composed by Thomas Mabiletsa[27] (Gallo Music Publishers)
Thomas Mabiletsa
Recorded in Johannesburg, c.1944; issued on Singer-Gallotone GE 943

TRACK 23
Zulu Piano Medley, No.2: Part 1
Composed by Thomas Mabiletsa[28] (Gallo Music Publishers)
Thomas Mabiletsa
Recorded in Johannesburg, c.1944; Singer, unissued

The great and famous early keyboard players in the *marabi*, vaudeville and jazz idioms included performers such as Ntebejana, Nine Fingers, Bridge Makeke, Emily Motsieloa, Sullivan Mphahlele, Jacob Moeketsi and Toko Khampepe. But none of the early performing styles of these musicians was preserved in solo recordings, and frequently not even in group recordings. It is one of the ironies of the South African recording industry that the first of the great pianists to make a solo recording (though with a light and barely audible drum-set accompaniment) was Thomas Mabiletsa, who, despite his prodigious talents, was little known in his own time.

---

26 Author's interview: Peter Rezant, Johannesburg 23 June 1985.
27 My attribution.
28 My attribution.

His two compositions entitled 'Zulu Piano Medley', partly reproduced here, give evidence of startling flair and originality. What we encounter in these recordings might, for a start, be described as a fusion of the stylistic principles of *marabi* and American 'stride' piano, a remarkable execution of bold polyrhythmic patterns, and a virtuoso performance style. There are no prototypes for precisely what Mabiletsa accomplishes here; but Meade Lux Lewis's 'Honky Tonk Train' (recorded by the American boogie-woogie pianist in 1929) makes an interesting comparison.

> **TRACK 24**
> *Izikhalo Zika Zuluboy*[29] [The Laments of Zuluboy]
> Composed by Solomon 'Zuluboy' Cele (Gallo Music Publishers)
> **Zuluboy and his Jazz Maniacs**
> Recorded in Johannesburg, May 1939; issued on Better XU 9
>
> **TRACK 25**
> *Tsaba Tsaba*
> Composed by Solomon 'Zuluboy' Cele (Gallo Music Publishers)
> **Zuluboy and his Jazz Maniacs**
> Recorded in Johannesburg, May 1939; issued on Better XU 9

Undoubtedly the most brilliant recorded examples of early South African big-band swing, these two pieces were also hugely popular in their day. And these recordings are of great historical importance in another sense: they are the first recordings the legendary Jazz Maniacs ever made, and the only ones to feature their charismatic leader, Solomon 'Zuluboy' Cele, who was murdered almost five years later. (Cele was also the composer of these pieces: or so, at least, his widow recalls.)[30]

Like Mabiletsa's 'Zulu Piano Medleys' – probably recorded in the year of Cele's death – these pieces are a strikingly original amalgam: this time a combination of harmonic features derived from *marabi*, with some of the stylistic traits of American big-band swing.

The title of the first piece suggests that, despite its bright character, at least on one level the piece is a kind of lament. And the sung portions, indeed, deal with an experience that was common to black workers, given the multitude of problems they faced in the cities: the song makes reference to a sense of wandering in the wilderness, of abandonment, of fear about the future. *Tsaba Tsaba* is the recording on the original 'flip'

---

29 The label misspells and abbreviates thus: *Izakalo Zika Z-Boy*.
30 Author's interview: Mrs. Solomon Cele, Johannesburg 18 March 1986.

side; as indicated earlier (Track 3), this is the name of a prominent dance style that was a successor to the *marabi* dance. And it has a sung portion that seems to continue the lament; now, however, wherever the wanderer travels, or rests, a lover offers solace.

Index

A[1]

Adams College, 24, 34, 35, 36
Adeler, Edgar, 52
African Darkies, 6
African Hellenics, 37
African Inkspots, 7
African Jazz Pioneers, 9
African Jazz *see Mbaqanga*
African Methodist Episcopal Church, 22
African Mineworkers' Union, 52
African Minstrels, 59
African music *see* Music, New Africanism
African National Congress, 36, 40, 56, 80
    and music, 52, 54
    and other political organisations, 56, 57
African National Congress Youth League, 57, 62
African Rhythmers, 37
African Theatrical Syndicate, 14
African Youngsters, 50
Africans' Club, 67
Africans' Own Entertainers, 19, 45, 58, 77
Afrikaans music, 27
Alexandrians, 65
All-African Convention, 52, 54
Allingham, Rob 3fn, 87fn
Amanzimtoti Players *see* Amanzimtoti Royal Entertainers
Amanzimtoti Royal Entertainers, 55, 58, 89, 93
American Board of Missions, 75
American influences on Black music *see* Black music, American
    influences on
ANC *see* African National Congress
Apartheid, 7, 8
    opposition, 9, 51, 56
    pass legislation, 12, 67-68
        for musicians, 67-70
Ashworth, A H, 34
At home, see Emakhaya
Aubuti Nkikho, 91

---

[1] The letters fn after a page reference refer to the footnote on that page.

Index

B

Bantu Glee Singers, 48, 90
Bantu Men's Social Centre, 12, 20
Bantu music *see* Traditional music
Bantu Revue Follies, 17, 58
Bayete, 9
Berlin, Irving, 20, 99
Berman, Charles, 44
Beusen, Tommy ('China'), 19, 45, 77
Bhengu, Peggy, 47
Bikitsha, Doc, 61
Black bands, relations with white bands *see* Music, relations between white/black musicians
Black music,
    American influences on, 4, 6, 7, 13-17, 22, 31, 41, 84, 91, 92
        from films, 20-21, 41
        from records, 18-19, 41
    fusion of American and traditional styles, 4, 6, 7, 9, 11, 23
    missionary influences on, 18, 22
Black nationalism *see* New Africanism
Black working class *see* Working class
Blue Dams, 50
Blue Lagoon Club, 43
BMSC *see* Bantu Men's Social Centre
Boon-Town, 38
Brand, Dollar *see* Ibrahim, Abdullah
Brass bands, 30, 63
    influences on African music, 31, 32-33
Brenner, Miss, 34
Broadcast music *see* msakazo music
Broadway Babies, 47
Broadway Stars, 37
Brother Nkikho, see Aubuti Nkikho
Brunswick Gramophone House, 87
Bunche, Ralph, 67
Burchmore, Eileen, 35

C

Caluza, Reuben, 51, 90
    songs/recordings, 45, 48, 84
    spirituals, 22
    traditional music, 24

        training people to play/sing/dance, 36
Cape Malay music, 27
Cele, Solomon 'Zuluboy', 2, 16, 62, 100
Chain Covers, see *iChain Covers*
Champion, A W G, 51
Chappel-Chappel S A, 99
Choirs, 4, 5, 18, 58, 80
Class culture, 3, 9, 11-12, 25, 34, 36
Clegg, Johnny, 9
Close harmony style *see Marabi*, style
Coloured musicians, 50, 52, 53, 94-95
Come on everybody, see Woza we Mzala
Communist Party, 51-52, 53, 56
Concert and Dance, 6, 12, 52
    aims, 25, 31, 36
    black American cultural influences on, 13-14, 22, 23
    culture, 37, 38
    New Africanism, 57-58
    venues, 12-13
Concert and Dance *see also* Jazz; Minstrelsy; Vaudeville
Congress of South African Trade Unions, 5, 9
Coon songs *see* Minstrelsy
COSATU *see* Congress of South African Trade Unions
Curfew regulations *see* Apartheid, pass legislation

D

Dangerous Blue Girls, 47
Darktown Negroes, 6
Darktown Strutters, 6, 20, 77, 89
    organisational links, 50
    role of women, 48
    social role, 41, 42
Davashe, Sherwood (Mackay), 37
Davis, Reuben E, 33-34
Dem Darkies, 50
Dhlomo, Herbert, 28, 44, 56
Dhlomo, R R R, 75-76, 80, 81, 83
Dixie Rag Lads, 50
Double Quartette, 51, 90
Dube, Frederick, 36
Dube, John, 36
Dube, Marie, 36
Dyani, Johnny, 7

Index

E

E Qonce, 62
E-Mtata, 62
Easton, M 35
eBhayi, 92
eGoli, 91
Emakhaya, 90
Emily, 88
Equality of blacks to whites shown through music *see* Music, social role
Ethnic identity, 8, 30, 58
Evelina, 94

F

Famous Broadway Entertainers, 50
Films, influence on black music *see* Black music, American influences on, from films
First Train, see *Stimela No. 1*
Fish and Chips, 62
Flying Birds, 79
Folk music *see* Traditional music

G

Gallo Music Publishers, 3, 95-98, 99, 100
Gashe, Boet, 6
Gay Gaeities, 16
Ghommaliedjies, 9, 27
Ginger Girls, 47
Goldberg, Mr, 34
'Gossip Pen' *see* Kuzwayo, Godfrey
Grinter, Miss, 35
Groenewald, Sonny, 94
Group Areas Act (1950), 7
Gumede, Willie, 98
Gwangwa, Jonas, 7

H

Hall, C W, 33
Hampton Jubilee Singers, 22
Harlem Babies, 13fn
Harlem Crazy Steppers, 47
Harlem Swingsters, 6, 61-62

Harmonic structure of *Marabi*, *see Marabi*, style
Harmony Kings, 6, 52
Healdtown Institution, 34
Heat Wave, 99
Hertzog Bills, 54, 56
Highbricks, 6, 89
Hot Lips Dance Band, 97
Hot Sparks, 47

I

Ibrahim, Abdullah, 7
iChain Covers, 95
ICU *see* Industrial and Commercial Workers' Union
Ideological campaign against *marabi see Marabi*, ideological campaign
I'm Blue without you, 44
In Johannesburg, *see* 'eGoli'
In Port Elizabeth, *see eBhayi*
indlamu, 60, 61
Industrial and Commercial Workers' Union, 50-51, 55
International Library of African Music, 3
Iqilika, 77-78
Isicathamiya, 4-5, 9
Isicathamiya, *see also* Working class
Izikhalo Zika Zuluboy, 100

J

Jabavu, D D T, 42-43, 82
Jazz, 8, 9-10
    American influences on, 13-16, 17, 23, 31, 39, 84, 85
    attitude to by middle class *see* Middle class, attitude
    culture, 2, 11, 17-18, 39-41, 80
    definition, 22-23
    history, 1-3
    New Africanism, 55-62, 86
    organisational links, 9, 50-51, 52
    pathologised, 80-81
    politicisation of, 8, 9, 11, 38
    relationship with Vaudeville, 11, 12-13
    repression of,
        on basis of class and gender, 74-86
        on basis of race, 63-74
    role of women, 46, 47-48
    social role, 8, 39, 50

      social role *see also* Music, social role
      songs/recordings, 93-101
      traditional music influences on, 23, 25, 39
Jazz *see also* Marabi; *Mbaqanga*
Jazz Maniacs 6, 13, 13fn, 28, 37, 68
Jazz Maniacs,
      American influences on, 15, 16, 19
      and *marabi*, 29, 34, 60
      and *mbaqanga*, 61
      musical training, 30, 35
      organisational links, 52
      relations with white musicans, 70
      role of women, 47, 48
      social role, 43
      songs/recordings, 100
      use of name, 73-74
Jazz Revellers Band, 6, 94-95
Johannesburg African Choral Society, 48
Johannesburg Musicians' Union, 71
Joint Committee of the Non-European Trade Unions, and music, 52
Jubilation, 37
Jubilation and Nice, 16
Jubilee singers, 4, 22

K

Kadalie, Clements, 51, 55
Kgokong, L 47
Khampepe, Toko, 17, 58, 99
Khanya, 91
Khumalo, Hope, 34, 47-48
Kimberley Amateur Entertainers, 17
Kippies, 9
Klaaste, Sol, 34
Kubik, Gerhard, 26
Kuzwayo, Godfrey, 48, 57-58
Kwela, 7
Kwenane, Emily, 16, 37

L

Lady Mine, 38
Lady Porcupine *see* Phahlane, Johanna ('Giddy')
Ladysmith Black Mambazo, 5

Laments of Zuluboy, see Izikhalo Zika Zuluboy
Lembede, Anton, 62
Letanke, D S, 67
Liberal reform movement, 74-75, 82
Liberal view in music *see* Music, liberal view
Light, see Khanya
Liquor Amendment Act (1934), 72
Liquor, role of in *Marabi, see Marabi*, and role of illegal liquor
Literacy, relevance in musical training *see* Musical training, and literacy
Log Cabin Club, 43, 70
Louter, George, 34
Lucky Stars, 58, 69, 70

M

Mabiletsa, Thomas, 97, 99-100
Mabuza, 98
McAdoo, Orpheus, 4, 22
McBein, Kenneth, 16
McGregor, Chris, 7
Madcaps, 47
Mad-Joe, 37
Mahlathini, 8
Majola, Ndaba, 54
Majuba, 62
Makeba, Miriam, 88
Makeke, Bridge, 99
Makhanya, Lindi, 19-20, 35, 48, 53, 80
Makhanya, Nimrod, 90
makwaya, 75
Mancoe, John, 54
Mandela, Nelson, 62
Manhattan Brothers, 2, 7
Manning, Charles, 74
Manson, Mrs, 34
Manyosi, Edward, 37
Marabi, 3, 5-6, 7, 34, 65-66
    attitude to by middle class *see* Middle class, attitude to
    definition, 25-26
    demise, 66, 70
    ideological campaign against, 74-79
    influence of traditional music, 26-27
    and *mbaqanga*, 61
    melodies, 26-27

    repression of, 64-65, 66
    and role of illegal liquor, 5, 26, 32, 63, 65, 66, 67, 72, 77, 94
    songs used as anti-*marabi*, 77-79
    songs/recordings, 6, 88, 93-96
    style, 5, 7, 26-27, 60, 89, 90, 93, 97
    and swing *see* Swing, and *marabi*
    and working class, 9, 26, 29, 75
Marabi cycle *see Marabi*, style
Marabi No. 2 Jive, 97
Marabi, *see also* Jazz; Working class
Marivate, Daniel, 24
Martin, Roy, 44
Masekela, Hugh, 7
Masinya Kids, 18
Masoleng, Johannes 'Koppie', 20, 35
Mass resistance movement *see* African National Congress
Matshikiza, Todd, 26, 37, 59, 61, 90
Mavimbela, John C P, 14, 54-55, 77, 91
Mayhew, Joyce, 35
Mbanjwa, Phillip, 35
Mbaqanga, 6, 7, 9, 60-62
mbaqanga, *see also* Jazz
Mbau, Gray, 61, 62
Mercury Stars, 14
Merry Blackbirds, 33fn, 37, 60, 65
Merry Blackbirds,
    American influences on, 6, 15, 16, 19, 21
    and jazz, 29, 85-86
    and *Marabi*, 95-96
    musical training, 34, 35
    organisational links, 52, 53
    relations with Pitch Black Follies, 13fn, 42
    relations with white musicians, 70-71
    role of women, 47, 48
    social role, 42, 43
    songs/recordings, 95-97, 99
Merry Makers, 35, 48
Merry Mascots, 50
Merry Mischiefs, 37
Mgijima, Enoch, 22
Middle class,
    attitude to Jazz/ragtime 1910's-1930's, 80-83
    attitude to Jazz/ragtime 1930's-, 84-86
    attitude to *marabi*, 6, 29, 32, 75-79, 90

attitude to traditional music, 23-24
  attitude to women, 82-83
  relations with working class, 12, 25, 74-75
  western values, 29, 31, 40, 56, 74, 75, 80, 81, 82
Middle class *see also* Working class
Middle class, White, 74
Midnight Follies, 14, 50
Mienaar, Henry, 37
Minedumps, see Ndunduma
Minstrels (group), 37
Minstrelsy, 4, 6
  influence on Jazz and Vaudeville, 18-19, 22
Minstrelsy *see also* Ragtime
Missionary influences on Black music *see see* Black music, missionary influences on
Mkhize, 98
Mkize, Victor, 35
Mmutle, Joseph, 30
Mochumi, Ernest 'Palm', 60, 65, 66, 68
Modikwe, Mac, 33fn
Modikwe's Band, 30, 33fn
Moeketsi, Jacob, 34, 70, 99
Mokgoro Band, 30
Mokone, Henry 'Japie', 44
Molema, S M, 47
Monare, Ignatius, 77, 91
Moral persuasion *see* Music, social role
Motsieloa Band, 47
Motsieloa Band *see also* Merry Blackbirds
Motsieloa, Emily, 36, 47, 95, 96-97, 99
Motsieloa, Griffiths, 2, 35, 36, 42, 53
  songs/recordings, 45, 77, 87, 88-89, 91, 97
Movietone Cabaret Girls, 47
Mphahlele, Es'kia, 17
Mphahlele, Sullivan, 14, 16, 99
Mrwebi, Gwigwi, 61
Msakazo music, 8
Mseleku, Bheki, 89
Mseleku, Wilfred, 89
Mseleku, William, 2, 55, 58, 89
Mtethwa, Esau, 58, 69
Mtethwa, Isaac, 58, 69
mube, see Isicathamiya

Index

Music,
    African *see* Music, New Africanism
    American influences on *see* Black music, American influences on
    contradictions, 39, 45-46, 49
    liberal view, 40-50, 69
    New Africanism, 7, 55-62
    organisational links, 50-55
    radical view, 50-55
    relations between black and white musicians, 70-73
    and repression,
        external, 63-74, 86
        internal, 74-86
    role of women, 46-49
    social role,
        financial benefits, 44, 45, 46
        to educate whites to blacks' equality, 8, 39-44, 56
Musical training, 15, 19-20, 73-74
    and literacy, 19-20, 26, 29, 33, 42
    mission schools, 30, 33, 34
    teachers,
        Black, 36-37, 38
        White, 33, 34, 35, 36
    Vaudeville, 35-36
My Heart is beating every hour for you, 44

N

Native Military Corps Brass Band, 31, 33
Natives (Urban Areas Act) 1923, 66
ndunduma, *see* Zulu music
Neo-traditional music, 26, 61, 89, 90
Neo-traditional music *see also* Marabi; Mbaqanga
New Africanism, 55-62, 84
New Africanism *see also* Jazz; Mbaqanga
New Paradise Club, 43
Ngamza, Sandy, 37
Ngubane, Jordan, 62
Nhlapo, Walter, 43, 61, 83
    American influences on Black music, 16, 17, 21
    Concert and Dance, 12, 14
    New Africanism in music, 57, 59, 60
Night curfew/passes *see* Apartheid, pass legislation
Nine Fingers, 6, 99
Nkandla Guitar Players, 94

Nlatseng, Jeremiah, 30
Ntebejana, 95
Ntebejana, 6, 88, 95, 99
Nthatisi, Florence K, 47

O

Oliphant, Babsy, 48
Oliphant, Eleanor, 48
'Ou Bles', 69, 70

P

Palladiums, 6
Pass laws *see* Apartheid, pass legislation
Petersen, Louis Radebe, 42
Petty bourgeois *see* Middle class
Phahlane, Johanna ('Giddy'), 35, 48-50, 55
Phillips, James, 53
Phillips, Ray, 20
Piliso, Ntemi, 19, 21
Pirate Coons, 4
Pitch Black Follies, 6, 77, 89
    American influences on, 16, 17-18, 20
    musical training, 35-36
    organisational links, 53
    role of women, 47
    social role, 43, 44
    songs/recordings, 90, 92
    relations with Merry Blackbirds *see* Merry Blackbirds, relations
Pixley's Mid-Night Follies, 14, 51
Plaatje, Sol, 20
Plaatje, V N, 47
Politics in music and towards an African style *see* Music, New Africanism
Pretorius, Marjorie, 13fn, 34, 37, 48
Pukwana, Dudu, 7

Q

Qua qa, 89
Quaker, Dale, 15
Qwabe, Petrus, 13fn

Index

R

Radebe, Mark, 24, 81, 85
Radebe, Snowy, 2, 90, 92
Radical view in music *see* Music, radical view
Ragtime, 18, 28, 80, 83, 84, 88, 94, 96-97
Ragtime *see also* Minstrelsy
Raven Girls, 47
Rayner's Big Six, 52
Record companies, 45-46
Records, influence on black music *see* Black music, American influences on, from records
Relocation *see* Removals policy
Removals policy, 7, 66
Repression of music *see* Music, and repression, external/internal
Resistance to government policies *see* Apartheid, opposition
Rezant, Peter, 42, 53, 80
    American influences on his music/band, 15, 16, 19, 21
    and his band Merry Blackbirds, 95, 96, 99
    and *marabi*, 29, 66
    musical training, 34, 35, 36
    relations with white musicians, 70-71, 72, 73
Rhythm Girls, 47
Rhythm Kings band, 6, 14, 54, 77, 91
Ritz Palais de Dance, 12-13
Robeson, Paul, 14, 41, 45, 53, 57
'Rollie Reggie' *see* Dhlomo, R R R

S

SABC *see* South African Broadcasting Corporation
Sabenza, 9
Sabi, Maurice, 37
Sakhile, 9
Salvation Army, 30
Sasithunywe Abazali, 79
Savuka, 9
Sbhinono, 93
Scogings, F, 51
Seme, Pixley ka Izaka, 51
Sentso, Wilfred, 45-46, 51, 52
    American influences on, 14, 16
    musical training, 36-37, 38
    New Africanism, 59, 60

Sentso, Wilfred *see also* Synco Schools
Separatist churches, 22
Sharpeville massacre, 7
shebeens, 26, 32, 64, 66
Shomang, Taai, 61
Shuping, Doris, 18
Silgee, Wilson 'King Force', 28-29, 72
    learning to play music, 30, 33, 34
Sililo, Edward ('Boetie Vark'), 13, 68-69
    and *marabi*, 26, 27, 29
    musical training, 19, 30, 33
    relations with white bands, 70, 73, 74
Sisulu, Walter, 62
Skylarks, 88
Slosberg, Bertha, 69, 70
Smart Girls, 47
Social role of music to educate whites to blacks' equality *see* Music, social role
Sonny's Jazz Revellers, 52, 53
South African Bantu Board of Music, 23, 39, 44
South African Broadcasting Corporation, 3, 5
    black radio services, 7-8
Spirituals, 4, 22, 57
Sponono, 94
Sponono with marabi, see *Sponono naMarabi*
Sponono naMarabi, 88
Squatter movements, 56
State of Emergency, 9
Stimela No. 1, 87
Stokvels, 31-32, 63, 64-65
Sunbeams, 50
Swing,
    American influences on, 6, 84, 86
    and *marabi*, 6, 7, 60, 61, 70, 100
Synco Down Beats Orchestra, 38, 43, 58-59
Synco Fans, 6, 16, 36, 38, 52
    New Africansim, 58-59
Synco Schools, 16, 37
Synco Schools *see also* Sentso, Wilfred

T

Tambo, Oliver, 62
The Making of a People, see The Progress of a Race
The Progress of a Race, 52
The Red Flag, 51
tikkie-draai, 27, 98
Toto, 6
Trade unions, 46, 56, 71
Traditional music, 9, 23-25, 26, 57
Transvaal African Eisteddfod, 31
Transvaal Musicians' Union, 71
Tsaba Tsaba, 100-101
Tsaba Tsaba ke No.1, 89
Tsaba-Baby-Tsaba, 38, 60
Tsaba-tsaba dance, 59-60, 89
Tula n'divile, see Xhosa music
Tyamzashe, Benjamin, 44

U

UDF *see* United Democratic Front
uMajaji, 96
United Democratic Front, 9
Universiity of Natal, Department of Music, 3

V

Van Rensburg, Teddy, 36
vastrap, 27, 98
Vaudeville, 3, 6, 12-13, 22, 39, 89
    American influences on, 6, 16, 17, 20-21, 91
    ethnicity, 58, 69
    New Africanism, 57, 58, 59, 62
    organisational links, 50, 51-52
    relationship with Jazz *see* Jazz, relationship with Vaudeville
    role of women, 46, 47, 48
    social role, 39, 41, 43, 50
    social role *see also* Music, social role
    songs/recordings, 87-92
    traditional influences on, 23, 25
Vaudeville *see also* Concert and Dance
Venues, 8, 9, 64, 66, 67, 70, 72
Vernacular in music *see* Music, New Africanism

Versatile Seven, 6
Vilakzi, B W, 40-41
Virginia Jubilee Singers, 4, 22

W

Waller, Fats, 14, 16
Wesleyan Church, 30
Western music, 80, 81-82
White musicians, 43-44, 52, 70-73
Whiteman, Paul, 84, 85
Wilberforce Institute Singers, 37
Willie Gumede's Swing Band, 98
Witwatersrand Native Labour Association, 31
Women, attitudes towards, 46-47, 48, 49-50, 82-83
Women, role in music *see* Music, role of women
Working class, 4-5, 74
    music culture, 5-6, 7, 11, 12, 25, 26, 29, 30-31, 38, 39, 64, 75
    politicisation of, 9, 40, 56
Working class *see also* Middle class
Working class, Zulu *see Isicathamiya*
Woza we Mzala, 97

X

Xhosa music, 27, 32, 64
Xuma, A B, 36, 51, 52
Xuma, Madie Hall, 52

Y

Yellow Coons, 4
Yengwa, M B, 80

Z

Zikali, W P, 95
Zonophone label, 17
Zulu music, 17, 27, 28, 64, 90
Zulu Piano Medley, No. 1/2, 99-100
Zuluboy and his Jazz Maniacs *see* Jazz Maniacs